ALLEN COUNTY PUBLIC LIBRARY

D0662789

**DO NOT REMOVE
CARDS FROM POCKET**

8-96

**ALLEN COUNTY PUBLIC LIBRARY
FORT WAYNE, INDIANA 46802**

You may return this book to any agency, branch,

or bookmobile of the Allen County Public Library.

DEMCO

THORSONS
PRINCIPLES
OF

BUDDHISM

KULANANDA

Thorsons
An Imprint of HarperCollinsPublishers

Allen County Public Library
900 Webster Street
PO Box 2270
Fort Wayne, IN 46801-2270

Thorsons
An Imprint of HarperCollins*Publishers*
77–85 Fulham Palace Road
Hammersmith, London W6 8JB
1160 Battery Street
San Francisco, California 94111–1213

Published by Thorsons 1996

10 9 8 7 6 5 4 3 2 1

© Kulananda 1996

Kulananda asserts the moral right to
be identified as the author of this work

A catalogue record for this book
is available from the British Library

ISBN 1 85538 508 2

Printed in Great Britain by
HarperCollinsManufacturing Glasgow

All rights reserved. No part of this publication may be
reproduced, stored in a retrieval system, or transmitted,
in any form or by any means, electronic, mechanical,
photocopying, recording or otherwise, without the prior
permission of the publishers.

FOR MY PARENTS
SYDNEY AND EDELE CHASKALSON

CONTENTS

ACKNOWLEDGEMENTS

Many streams have flowed into the making of this book. It contains nothing original. I have drawn without stint from the writings and lectures of my friends and my teacher. In particular, Andrew Skilton's *Concise History of Buddhism*, Vessantara's *Meeting the Buddhas*, and Kamalasila's *Meditation, the Buddhist Way to Tranquillity and Insight* have all been helpful, as has Stephen Batchelor's *The Awakening of the West*.

Without the writings and works of my teacher, Sangharakshita, I'd have nothing worthwhile to say. If this book has any merit, it is all due to him. I have drawn on all his books, most particularly *The Three Jewels*, *Vision and Transformation*, *A Guide to the Buddhist Path* and *The Ten Pillars of Buddhism*.

Sangharakshita, Kamalasila and Nagabodhi read the manuscript and made many helpful comments. Vishvapani took on extra work to give me the time to write. I am grateful to them all.

INTRODUCTION

Over half the world's population lives in countries which have been significantly influenced by Buddhist ideas and practices, yet from the time of the Buddha – half a millenium before the founding of Christianity – right up until the middle part of the twentieth century, the vast majority of Westerners knew almost nothing about it. Around the middle of the twentieth century, however, this began to change and Buddhism is now said to be the fastest growing religion in the West.

At a time when we are faced with a stark choice between the increasing demands of consumerism on the one hand, and religions which strain our credulity on the other, more and more men and women are turning to Buddhism as a way of discovering those human and spiritual values so lacking in the world today.

But what is Buddhism? We are used to thinking of religion as being somehow about a belief in God, in one or another of the many guises in which he is seen, but there is no God in Buddhism. Is it then simply a philosophy – a way of thinking about the world, or a way of leading a more ethical life? Or is it a kind of psychotherapy – a way of helping us to come to terms with ourselves and with the dilemmas which life constantly throws up? Buddhism contains all of these to some extent, but it is also very much more.

Buddhism asks us to reconsider our usual preconceptions of what is meant by religion. It deals with truths which go entirely beyond the merely rational, unfolding a transcendental vision of reality which altogether surpasses all our usual categories of thought. The Buddhist path is a way of spiritual training which leads, in time, to a direct, personal apprehension of that transcendental vision.

Every one of us has the capacity to be clearer, wiser, happier and freer than we currently are. We have the capacity to penetrate directly to the heart of reality – to come to know things as they really are. The teachings and methods of Buddhism ultimately have one goal alone: to enable us to fully realize that potential for ourselves.

Over the course of its long history, Buddhism spread to all the countries of Asia. Wherever it alighted, the interaction between the indigenous local culture and the newly arrived teachings of the Buddha wrought profound effects on both. In many cases Buddhism ignited a cultural renaissance. In some situations, as in Tibet, it was even the harbinger of culture. And as it moved, Buddhism too changed, adapting wherever it went to local cultural conditions. Thus, today, we have the Buddhisms of Sri Lanka, Thailand, Burma, Vietnam, Cambodia, Laos, Tibet, China, Mongolia, Russia and Japan; and within these a bewildering variety of schools, sects and sub-sects. Where in all this variety is Buddhism itself? What do all these different approaches have in common?

What they most have in common is their ancestral origin. They are all branches, leaves and flowers which have grown out from the trunk of early Indian Buddhism. They all look back to the Buddha and they all accept and propound the Buddha's original teachings, although with very different emphases.

To understand the fundamentals of Buddhism, therefore, it is necessary to get back as close as we can to the Buddha himself. We can do this by looking into the earliest texts and seeing what they have to say for us today. This is not to reject later developments. Buddhists in the West today stand as heirs to the whole Buddhist tradition. We can admire, respect and make practical use of elements of Japanese Soto Zen as much as we can elements of Tibetan Vajrayana or Thai Theravada. But to understand the tradition *as a whole* we need to go back to its roots.

Most of the basic teachings in this book go back to early Indian Buddhism. I therefore hope that there is little here that Buddhists of different traditional allegiance would take issue with. For the same reason, I have generally confined myself to the early Indian canonical languages in the few cases where I need to describe Buddhist technical terms, using either Pali or Sanskrit as seems most appropriate in context. (This not being a scholarly work, I have omitted diacritical marks.)

The principal intention of this book is to introduce the general reader to the broad range of the Buddhist tradition by bringing out some of its most essential (and therefore most common) elements, and to show how the fundamental teachings of Buddhism have a significance which transcends their historical origins. Above all I hope it encourages some readers to try these out for themselves. Books are very useful, but if one really wants to know what Buddhism is about, one must try it out in practice. Even the most gifted writer cannot describe the flavour of an orange, and in the same way no book can ever capture the essence of Buddhist practice.

'Just as the great ocean has one taste, the taste of salt,' the Buddha said, 'so my teaching has one flavour – the flavour of liberation.'

THE BUDDHA

'**B**uddha' is not a name, it is a title, meaning 'One Who is Awake' – awake to the highest reality, to things as they really are. And one becomes a Buddha through achieving Enlightenment – a state of transcendental insight into the true nature of reality. There have been many Enlightened individuals throughout Buddhist history, but the term 'the Buddha' is usually used to refer to one particular Enlightened individual, Siddhartha Gautama, the founder of the Buddhist religion, the first person in our era to tread the path to Enlightenment.

Siddhartha was born in about 485 BCE (Before Common Era) in Lumbini, near the town of Kapilavastu in the area below the foothills of the Himalayas which spans the current Nepalese border with India. It was a time of great political change. In the central Ganges basin, not very far to the south, powerful new monarchies were emerging which were gradually swallowing up the older, clan-based republics. One or two republics, however, still held out, and it was into one of these, that of the Shakyans, that Siddhartha Gautama was born.

Siddhartha's family belonged to the warrior class, and his father was a member of the ruling oligarchy. Later tradition, knowing only the monarchies which soon usurped the earlier republics, dubbed Siddhartha a 'prince', and his father,

Suddhodana, the 'king'; but whatever his correct designation, we know that Suddhodana was rich and powerful and that the young Siddhartha led a privileged life.

At his birth, a seer predicted that the young boy was destined for either political or spiritual empire (his name, Siddhartha, means 'he whose aim will be accomplished'). The legendary biographies tell that in his early life his father, wishing that his handsome and accomplished son should choose a life of political rather than spiritual empire, sought to attach him to the advantages of wealth and power by providing him with every available luxury, and keeping him sheltered from the harsher facts of the world about him. He arranged for Siddhartha's marriage to a beautiful and refined young woman, Yashodhara, and she bore him a son, Rahula.

But Siddhartha began to develop an acute sense of dissatisfaction. He sensed the hollowness which underlay his superficially comfortable life, and he was unable to brush this feeling aside. His innate integrity wouldn't allow him to pretend that everything was as it should be. He was driven to intellectual and spiritual exploration, seeking for answers which his privileged environment was unable to provide. This period of questioning is vividly expressed by the story of the four sights – four formative experiences which occurred to the young trainee-warrior whilst travelling abroad in his chariot.

The story goes that at the side of the road one day he caught his first ever sight of an old man, and thus realized, for the first time, the inevitable fact of old age. Similarly, he was confronted in turns by disease and by death. These experiences completely overwhelmed him. What was the point of living a life of ease and luxury when old age, disease and death were waiting in the wings – quietly biding their time before they came to claim him, his family and friends? Finally he saw a wandering mendicant, the sight of whom sowed in his mind the seed of the possibility that there was an alternative to the passive acceptance of old age, disease and death. But, at the same time, he saw that to embark on such a quest would require radical, even painful, action.

And so Siddhartha passed his early years – restless, worried by matters of profound existential concern and torn between the life for which ancestry had prepared him and the religious quest towards which his restless spirit propelled him. His insight into the inevitable facts of old age, disease and death, left him with an acute and ineradicable sense of the painful vacuity of the 'pleasures' and plottings of upper-class Shakyan life. Ancestral duty demanded that he join in, put his sense of the hollowness of things aside, and get on with the business of warriorship and government. Yet, at his core, where he was truest to himself, he knew that a life which denied the fundamentals of reality was not for him. He saw that he had two stark options: he could deny himself reality or he could deny himself family, luxury and power. He chose to seek reality, and at the age of 29, without the approval or even knowledge of his wife and father, he stole away from home, leaving behind wife, child, family and social status. He cut off his hair and beard, swapped his warrior garb for the rag robes of a religious mendicant, and began his search for truth and liberation.

It was an unsettled time. Rival kings, striving to establish ever larger kingdoms, were gradually absorbing and centralizing the earlier family- and tribe-oriented social structures. The old religion of the *Vedas* and its Brahminical priesthood was increasingly associated with these centralized governments, and a new class of religious practitioner was emerging. These were the wandering ascetics, who, dissatisfied with social conventions and with the empty ritualism of established religion, gave up their homes and social positions to wander at will in the world, living on alms and seeking spiritual liberation.

4   Siddhartha became a 'wanderer'.

He sought out the most famous spiritual teachers of his time, but soon surpassed them in spiritual attainment and, realizing that even the lofty heights to which they had led him didn't provide the answers he was looking for, he left each of them in turn and continued on his quest alone.

It was a commonly accepted belief at the time that one liberated the spirit by weakening the prison of the flesh, and for the next six years Siddhartha engaged in the practice of extreme religious austerities. He wore no clothes, didn't wash and went without food and sleep for increasingly long periods.

> All my limbs became like the knotted joints of withered creepers, my buttocks like a bullock's hoof, my protruding backbone like a string of balls, my gaunt ribs like the crazy rafters of a tumble-down shed. My eyes lay deep in their sockets, their pupils sparkling like water in a deep well. As an unripe gourd shrivels and shrinks in a hot wind, so became my scalp. If I thought, 'I will touch the skin of my belly', it was the skin of my backbone that I also took hold of, since the skin of my belly and my back met. The hairs, rotting at the roots, fell away from my body when I stroked my limbs.[1]

Renowned for the extent of his asceticism, his fame 'rang like a bell' throughout northern India, and he began to attract a following. But he was still not satisfied. Six years after leaving home, he was no nearer to resolving the fundamental questions of existence than he had been at the beginning of his quest. Realizing that his austerities had led him nowhere, despite his great name and reputation as a holy ascetic, Siddhartha had the moral courage to abandon his previous course. He began to eat in moderation, and his former disciples, scandalized by this backsliding, left him in disgust.

He was now completely alone. Family, clan, reputation, followers – all abandoned. All his attempts to break through the veil of ignorance had failed. Desolate, he didn't know which way to turn next. Only one thing was certain – he would not abandon his quest.

At this point a memory rose to the surface of his mind. When he was quite young, sitting in the shade of a rose-apple tree, he had watched his father ploughing. Relaxed by the slow, steady rhythm of the ox-team, content in the cool shade, he had spontaneously slipped into a concentrated meditative state – might that be the way to Enlightenment?

In this state of acute existential solitude, his determination unshaken, according to legend Siddhartha sat down under a tree with this declaration:

> Flesh may wither away, blood may dry up, but I shall not leave
> this seat until I gain Enlightenment!

For days and nights he sat there in meditation.

The legends present a vivid account of the existential struggle which Siddhartha was now engaged in. It was time for his confrontation with Mara, the Evil One – the archetypal embodiment of all that stands between us and the truth.

Seeing Siddhartha sitting thus determinedly in meditation, Mara shook with fright:

> He had with him his three sons – Flurry, Gaiety and Sullen Pride
> – and his three daughters – Discontent, Delight and Thirst. These
> asked him why he was so disconcerted in his mind. And he
> replied to them with these words: 'Look over there at that sage,
> clad in the armour of determination, with truth and spiritual
> virtue as his weapons, the arrows of his intellect drawn, ready to
> shoot! He has sat down with the firm intention of conquering my

realm. No wonder that my mind is plunged in deep despondency! If he should succeed in overcoming me, and should proclaim to the world the way to final beatitude, then my realm would be empty today. But so far he has not yet won the eye of full knowledge. He is still within my sphere of influence. While there is time I will therefore break his solemn purpose, and throw myself against him like the rush of a swollen river breaking against the embankment!'

But Mara could achieve nothing against the Buddha-to-be, and he and his army were defeated, and fled in all directions – their elation gone, their toil rendered fruitless, their rocks, logs, trees scattered everywhere. They behaved like a hostile army whose commander had been slain in battle. So Mara, defeated, ran away together with his followers. The great seer, free from the dust of passion, victorious over darkness's gloom, had vanquished him.[2]

Siddhartha sat calmly beneath the tree, allowing his mind to become still. Gradually, all the different currents of his psyche began to flow together. Steadily, his concentration increased. As it grew more and more focused, Siddhartha's mind became clearer and brighter. Not allowing anything to impede this process, Siddhartha let it grow and strengthen. On and on, deeper and deeper into meditation, his mind became clear as a blazing diamond, glowing with ever increasing brilliance. It was intensely pleasurable, but Siddhartha wasn't distracted by the pleasure – letting go of it, he entered states of increasingly profound equanimity.

Gradually, the bright rays of his concentrated mind began to light up the past. He remembered all the details of his past, back to his earliest childhood and then, suddenly, he saw back even further than that, and he began to recall his previous life. As his concentration deepened he saw further and further back – an endless stream of lives, arising and passing away in unceasing succession. Here he had been born, with this name, lived in that way, died at such an age and had been reborn in such a place – again and again, over and over. He saw each life in complete detail. On and on, the rhythm repeated unendingly. Birth, growth, disease and death; birth, growth, disease and death – an endless round.

Then the barriers which had divided him off from others fell away and he saw before him the lives of countless other beings, their struggles, successes and failures, and he felt the unfailing rhythm of their lives: birth and death, birth and death, birth and death – the timeless pulse of suffering humanity.

Siddhartha began to discern a pattern within this ceaseless flux of change. Those whose lives had been based in kindness and generosity were reborn in happy circumstances, those who gave way to greed and hatred were inevitably reborn in states of suffering. Watching life after life he found that he could predict the outcomes of people's actions. Those who spread happiness generated happy circumstances for themselves; those who caused pain and separation found themselves alone in a hostile world. It was so clear and yet, preoccupied with their petty dealings, people failed to see it.

Siddhartha began to identify each step of the process whereby the unending stream of birth and death took place. Birth and death followed from craving. It was their deep craving for existence which led beings from life to life in an endless round of suffering. With the ceasing of craving, birth, death and suffering also ceased. Having directly apprehended the link between craving and suffering, Siddhartha could no longer be misled into believing that craving could bring happiness in its train. This brought about a dramatic change in his being. All traces of his own craving died away. Birth and death dissolved. The limited, human personality 'Siddhartha' simply dropped away. All that was left was total, luminous clarity. Perfect understanding. Infinite freedom and unrestricted creativity.

In the final watch of that full moon night in May, complete Enlightenment had finally dawned. Siddhartha Gautama became the Buddha.

> And the moon, like a maiden's gentle smile, lit up the heavens, while a rain of sweet-scented flowers, filled with moisture, fell down on the earth from above.[3]

Siddhartha spent several weeks absorbing this profound experience. He pondered for some time whether or not he could make his discovery of Enlightenment known to others – it was so subtle. To penetrate into it required calm and great concentration, people were so caught up in their petty desires, getting and spending; so attached to family, friends, wealth and reputation.

Then, the legend runs, a celestial being appeared and begged him to teach, for there were some beings in the world 'with but little dust on their eyes' who were perishing for want of the teachings.

With the eye of his imagination, the Buddha surveyed all the beings in the world. He saw all living beings as a vast bed of lotus flowers. Some flowers were sunk deep in the mire, others had raised their heads to the level of the water, and yet others had risen quite above the water – though they had their roots in the mud they were reaching up towards the light. There *were* beings who would understand what he had to say. The Buddha decided to teach.

Leaving the place we now know as Bodh Gaya, he walked the hundred or so miles to Sarnath, near the ancient city of Varanasi, where some of his former disciples were staying in a deer park. As he approached they looked to one another in disgust – here was the backslider Gotama, the *former* recluse. What did *he* want? They were certainly not doing to receive *him* with respect. But as the Buddha approached they were so taken with his calm, radiant demeanour that they couldn't help but defer to him.

These were stubborn men. Hardened by years of asceticism, full-timers in the spiritual quest, they thought they had heard it all. But the Buddha seemed to be approaching life from an entirely new dimension. There was something inexplicably different about him. They got down to debate – tough, straight talking, going to the very heart of things. Their discussions went on for days. Every now and again someone would leave to beg alms for the others, and then return to the fray. The Buddha's conviction and confidence was absolute. He had found the skilful Middle Way to Enlightenment, a path leading between the extremes of hedonism and asceticism; nihilism and eternalism.

Finally, the ascetic Kaundinya broke through. He saw what the Buddha was driving at, not just intellectually – he had the same kind of experience that the Buddha had under the tree at Bodh Gaya. His attachment to his own limited personality dropped away and he, too, was now free from the bondage of craving.

The Buddha was delighted – 'Kaundinya knows!' he exclaimed, 'Kaundinya knows!' What the Buddha had discovered *could* be made known. If Kaundinya could understand, then others could too. Humanity *would* benefit from these teachings. Over the next few days the other ascetics also became Enlightened. Then a young man called Yasa came by. Engaging the Buddha in discussion, he was convinced of the truth of the teachings, and so brought his family and friends along to hear them. In this way a new spiritual community – a *Sangha* – came into being. Soon there were 60 Enlightened beings in the world, and the Buddha sent them out to teach 'for the welfare and happiness of the many, out of compassion for the world.'

For the next 45 years the Buddha wandered around northern India. Sometimes alone, sometimes accompanied by members of the growing community that was coming into being around him. As he wandered, he taught. Kings, courtesans, sweepers and householders; all kinds of people came to hear the Buddha teach. What he taught was the Dharma.

'Dharma' is a complex Sanskrit word (in Pali, the other main language of the ancient Indian Buddhist texts, it is 'Dhamma'). It can mean law, or way, or truth. Here, it stands for all those teachings and practices which lead one towards Enlightenment. Over time, the Dharma which the Buddha taught came to be systematized. Repeated for hundreds of years in a purely oral tradition (the Buddha himself, like most of his kinsmen, was probably illiterate) the Dharma eventually formed the basis of an immense literary tradition, but at the start of it all there was just the Buddha, wandering about, trying to get people to see things more clearly, freely sharing his wisdom for the sake of all living beings, helping others to move towards the transcendental insight which he himself had attained.

Over the course of his life, the Buddha's fame as a teacher spread throughout northern India, an area of fifty thousand square miles, encompassing seven different nations. He was known as Shakyamuni – 'the Sage of the Shakya Clan' – and there was an immense general interest in what he had to say. Enlightened at about 35, he lived until about 80, and all of those 45 years were given over to teaching. Except in the rainy season, when he and whatever followers were with him retired into retreat, he walked the hot and dusty roads, passing through villages and cities, living on alms, taking only what was freely offered to him, and addressing himself to all who wanted to hear what he had to say, irrespective of sex, caste, vocation or religion. Amongst his followers were two of the principal kings of the region, members of most of the leading republican families, and some of the wealthiest merchants. On his travels he came into close personal contact with wandering ascetics, peasants, artisans, shop-keepers and robbers. People of all castes poured into his Sangha, where they lost their separate designations of caste and class – becoming simply 'followers of the Buddha'.

Wherever he could, the Buddha tried to help people to see things as they really are, responding to every situation out of the depths of his wisdom and compassion. One day, for example, a woman called Kisa Gotami came to see him. Her child had died and she was distraught. Clutching the dead baby to her breast, she rushed about, looking for that medicine which would restore the child to life. Thrusting the dead child up at the Buddha, she wailed – 'Please, please! Give me medicine for my baby!'

'Very well,' said the Buddha, 'but first you must bring me a mustard seed.'

A mustard seed! How easy!

'But,' the Buddha added, 'it must come from a house where no-one has died.'

Kisa Gotami rushed off to beg her mustard seed. She dashed from house to house. People were very willing to help her, but whenever she asked 'Has anyone ever died in this house?' the answer was the same. 'Alas, yes. The dead are many and the living are few.'

Kisa Gotami was utterly beside herself. Where was she going to find the mustard seed she so badly needed? As she passed from house to house the message gradually began to sink in. Death comes to all. There is no getting away from it. She returned to the Buddha and laid down her dead child. 'I know

now that I am not alone in this great grief. Death comes to all.'

Kisa Gotami joined the Sangha and, in due course, became Enlightened.

Another time the Buddha found himself in a part of the country which was being terrorized by a bandit called Angulimala – 'Finger Necklace' – who, after killing his victims, had the gruesome habit of cutting off one of their fingers and adding it to a string of them which he wore around his neck. His ambition was to acquire a hundred such fingers. At the time we are speaking of he had 98, and he was so desperate to reach his goal that he was just beginning to think that he might have to kill his old mother, who lived with him and did the cooking.

As the Buddha came to the area where Angulimala lived, the terrified villagers begged him not to go any further, for the danger was immense. But the Buddha quietly ignored their pleas and set out at a steady pace, calm and alert as ever.

Angulimala saw a figure approaching. 'Who dares to come like this into my territory, so calm and steady?' He was used to people trying to keep under cover, rushing anxiously through. 'Very well. Finger number 99 coming up!' And he grabbed for his sword and set off in pursuit of the Buddha. But however fast he ran he couldn't keep up with the Buddha, who was walking at his usual steady pace. This so intrigued Angulimala that he couldn't help but call out 'Hey! Stop, monk, stop!' The Buddha turned.

'I have stopped, Angulimala, you stop too.'

'How can you lie like that? And you a holy man!' exclaimed an indignant Angulimala. 'I can't catch up with you even though I am running as fast as I can. How can you say that you are standing still?'

'I am standing still, because I am standing in Nirvana,' the Buddha replied. 'You are moving, because you are going round and round on the Wheel of Rebirth,' replied the Buddha.

Angulimala was so moved by the Buddha's calm demeanour and compassionate attitude that he gave up violence and begged to be allowed to become one of the Buddha's followers. He joined the Sangha and made rapid spiritual progress.

One day a king came to see the Buddha. They got into discussion and the question arose as to who was the happier, the king or the Buddha. 'Of course I'm happier,' said the king, 'I've got palaces, wives, courtiers, wealth, armies, horses and elephants. I have power, fame – anything I want. What do you have? A robe, a begging bowl, a few scruffy followers ...'

'Tell me,' asked the Buddha, 'could you sit here for an hour, doing nothing at all, fully alert, enjoying complete happiness?'

'Er ... I suppose I could, ' replied the king.

'And could you sit here for six hours – without moving – enjoying complete and perfect happiness?'

'Ah ... that would be rather difficult,' said the king.

'And could you sit here for a day and a night, without moving, being perfectly happy, all the time?'

The king admitted that would be beyond him.

'But I can sit here for seven days and seven nights, without stirring, all the time enjoying complete and perfect happiness,' said the Buddha. 'Therefore, I think I am more happy than you.'

And so the Sangha grew and the Dharma spread far and wide. But the Buddha wasn't interested in disciples simply for the sake of a large following. Nor did he want people to follow him out of blind faith. He wanted people to check his teachings out in practice. To try them out and see if they actually worked for them.

Once a group of young men from the Kalama clan came to visit him. They were confused as to the rival claims of the different spiritual teachers of the day. They all seemed to make contradictory claims. How were they to choose between them? The Buddha replied:

> Do not go by hearsay nor by what is handed down by others. Nor by what people say, nor by what is stated on the authority of your traditional teachings. Do not go by reasoning, nor by inferring, nor by argument as to method, nor by reflection on and approval of an opinion; nor out of respect – thinking that a teacher must be deferred to. But, when you know of yourselves: 'These teachings are not good; they are blameworthy; they are condemned by the wise: these teachings, when followed out and put in practice, conduce to loss and suffering' – then reject them.[4]

So, yes, we have to refer to people wiser than ourselves. Teachings must, after all, be taught, and some 'are condemned by the wise', but nonetheless we must test everything we hear in the crucible of our own practice and experience. If teachings lead to happiness and gain, we can accept them. If they lead to loss and suffering, they must be rejected.

Finally, at the age of 80, his body worn out and racked with pain, the Buddha made one final teaching tour, giving all his friends and followers one final chance to ask him any questions they might have about the teaching. To the last he was completely aware and concerned only for the welfare of others. A wanderer called Subhadra came to see him on his death-bed, and Ananda, the Buddha's companion, turned him away, not wanting the Buddha to be disturbed at such a time. But the Buddha insisted on talking with him and Subhadra, soon convinced of the truth of the Dharma, joined the Sangha.

Then the Buddha asked if any of the assembled Sangha had any doubts or questions about his teaching. With typical thoughtfulness, he allowed that those who were too embarrassed to ask for themselves might do so through a friend. The answer was a resounding silence. The Buddha had made the Dharma perfectly clear. Seeing this, he gave a final exhortation to his followers: 'All conditioned things are impermanent! With mindfulness, strive!' And with that he entered into a state of deep meditation and passed away.

For most of his teaching career, the Buddha was accompanied by his cousin and close friend Ananda, who is reputed to have had a prodigious memory. All the doctrinal stories in the Buddhist scriptures are attributed to him, for apparently he remembered all the different occasions on which the Buddha taught, and recounted them in full to a council of the Sangha which was called after the Buddha's death, thus laying the foundations of an oral tradition which preserved the teachings until they began to be committed to writing several hundred years later.

For the last two and a half thousand years the Buddha's teachings have enabled countless men and women to achieve liberation – 'the heart's release'. In the Deer Park in Sarnath, with his former ascetic followers, the Buddha set rolling the Wheel of the Dharma. Since then it has rolled on down the centuries – through India and Sri Lanka, Burma, Thailand, Cambodia, Laos, Nepal, Tibet, China, Vietnam, Korea and Japan. Millions upon millions of people have been deeply affected by the Teaching. Wherever it went it wrought profound personal, social and cultural change.

But what exactly is the Dharma? And what use can it be – a body of teaching which was propounded two and a half thousand years ago in India?

16   *References*

1) *Majjima-Nikaya* 245–6. Quoted in Garry Thomson's
   Reflections On the Life of the Buddha, Buddhist Society,
   London, 1983.

2) From Canto 11 of the *Buddhacarita*, or 'The Acts of the
   Buddha', by the first century Indian poet Ashvaghosha.
   Edward Conze, *Buddhist Scriptures*, Penguin, 1959.

3) Ibid.

4) *Anguttara-Nikaya*, 1.188. F.L. Woodward, *Some Sayings of
   the Buddha*, Oxford University Press, 1973.

THE DHARMA

After the Buddha's death his followers correlated all of his major teachings. In time these were set to verse, committed to memory and passed down from generation to generation in what must be one of the most magnificent episodes of oral tradition in human history, for the 'literature' thus transmitted was immense. Similar, in its oral nature, to the Greek Homeric Epics, it was much more extensive and more highly organized. When finally committed to writing, as it began to be around about the first century BCE, it eventually came to occupy what in modern terms would be a small library.

Having eventually been written down, in Pali, Sanskrit or other variants of Indian contemporary language, the Dharma – the teachings of the Buddha – developed and expanded. New material was brought in, and a vast canonical literature comprising records of the Buddha's discourses and discussions, stories, parables, poems, and analyses gradually grew up.

Rather than a single, pleasantly portable Bible, the Buddhist canonical literature is very extensive. Traditionally it is spoken of as the *Tripitaka*, the Three 'Baskets', perhaps harking back to a time when texts were kept in that way. There is the *Sutra-Pitaka*, the collection of discourses either spoken by the Buddha or by one or another of his Enlightened disciples; the *Vinaya-Pitaka*, which contains accounts of the development of the early Sangha, as well as the monastic code; and the *Abhidharma-Pitaka*, a compendium of Buddhist psychology and philosophy.

As the Buddhist tradition split into different schools, each had its own version of the *Tripitaka*, although there are very substantial overlaps between them. Versions of the Canon which were written in Sanskrit have mainly been lost, and now exist for the most part only in Chinese, Japanese and Tibetan translation, whereas the Pali Canon was preserved intact in the language in which it first came to be written.

With the passing of time, the tree of the Dharma has sprouted new branches and stems as great Enlightened masters brought their own particular insights to bear on it. Apart from its existence in literary form, there are also oral lineages of Dharma transmission, from master to disciple, and even purely mental lineages, where the nature of reality is 'pointed out' in direct communication, unmediated by texts or liturgy. The Dharma can be transmitted in any way that results in people being brought closer to an understanding of ultimate truth.

One of the most common ways in which the Dharma has been transmitted is by way of the 'lists' with which Buddhism abounds. Taken together, these form a vast interlocking matrix of both doctrine and method which contain the whole of the Dharma. Taken singly, each list contains within it the seeds of all the rest, for the Dharma is like a vast jewelled net, where every jewel in the net perfectly contains and reflects the image of every other jewel.

The list of lists is immense – there are, to name but a very few, those which between them make up the Thirty-Seven *Bodipakkhiya-Dhammas* – 37 'Teachings Pertaining to Enlightenment'. These are: Four Foundations of Mindfulness; the Four Exertions; the Four Bases of Psychic Power; the Five Spiritual Faculties; the Five Spiritual Powers; the Seven

Factors of Enlightenment and the Noble Eightfold Path.
Opaque as these will doubtless seem to the newcomer, these lists are in fact an invaluable treasury of spiritual teaching.

Perhaps the most popular of all of these sorts of teaching is the teaching of the Four Noble Truths and the Noble Eightfold Path, which formed a major part of the Buddha's first ever discourse on the Dharma.

THE FOUR NOBLE TRUTHS

As I have described, the Buddha embarked on the quest for Enlightenment because he was deeply dissatisfied. He'd seen the inevitability of suffering old age, disease and death come to everyone, and he couldn't just shut his eyes and lose himself in the shallow diversions we usually employ to avoid confronting the starker realities of life.

The Buddha saw that life was marked with one universal quality: it was never entirely satisfying. The Pali term for this quality of unsatisfactoriness is *dukkha*. Etymologically, it is linked to the idea of an ill-fitting cartwheel – something which doesn't run smoothly, which is bumpy and uncomfortable. It describes the way things never come out quite right. Our lives contain pleasure and pain, gain and loss, happiness and sadness. But what they don't contain is ultimate, final satisfaction. We never quite get all we're looking for. This, the Buddha saw, is the fundamental human predicament.

In addressing himself to the problem of *dukkha*, the Buddha adopted a classical ancient Indian medical formula: a disease is diagnosed; its cause is identified; a cure is determined; a remedy is prescribed. Applying this analysis to the fundamental human predicament, the Buddha arrived at the Four Noble Truths.

The First Noble Truth identifies the problem. 'There is *dukkha*' – unsatisfactoriness.

Because we are never satisfied, we chase after experience. Constantly seeking satisfaction from the intrinsically unsatisfying, like hamsters in a wheel, we chase round and round, getting nowhere. Gain turns to loss, happiness gives way to sadness. We always seem to think that final, complete satisfaction is just around the corner. 'If only I can do this or get that, then everything will be fine and I'll be happy ever after.' But in reality it's never like that. The wheel just keeps on turning.

The Second Noble Truth asserts that the cause of *dukkha* is craving.

We are never satisfied because we have a fundamental disposition towards craving. No matter what we get, no matter how much or how good, we always want more, or we want something else, or we want it to stop.

Between them, craving and its counterpart, aversion, set the shape and boundaries of our personality – 'I am the person who drives such and such a car; shops in such and such a place; lives in such and such a neighbourhood; wears such and such clothes ...' Thus we create our fragile identities. But the structure is unstable. Things always change. Life flows on and we find ourselves caught up in a remorseless process of continually having to reconstruct ourselves – 'I like this, I want that; I don't like this, I don't want that' over and over, unendingly. Such is the un-Enlightened human predicament – endless unsatisfactoriness, driven by craving.

The Third Noble Truth asserts that with the cessation of craving unsatisfactoriness also ceases.

This is what the Buddha saw on the night of his Enlightenment. Having seen so clearly that the whole of existence, the endless round of birth and death, is driven by insatiable craving, he could no longer live as if craving would ever produce the final satisfaction with which it constantly enticed. The bonds of craving dropped away, and with it all that had limited and constricted him – he was free.

The Fourth Noble Truth asserts that there is a path which leads to the cessation of craving: the Noble Eightfold Path.

THE NOBLE EIGHTFOLD PATH

Translators usually render the Pali word *samma*, which is pre-fixed to all of the eight limbs or aspects of the Noble Eightfold Path, as 'right', but this can give the wrong impression, as if there were a simple 'right' way of doing things as opposed to the 'wrong' way, and that one could easily get the path 'right' and have done with it. But the Buddhist path isn't quite so simply divided into 'right' and 'wrong'. It is more develop-mental than that, for it is a path of practice, where there is always room for improvement. Rather than 'right' we can use the word 'perfect'.

The Noble Eightfold Path therefore consists of Perfect Vision, Perfect Emotion, Perfect Speech, Perfect Action, Perfect Livelihood, Perfect Effort, Perfect Awareness and Perfect *Samadhi*.[1]

The Path isn't traversed in simple consecutive steps. We don't start with vision, move on to emotion, then speech, action, livelihood etc. Rather, one works in different ways on different aspects all the time. But there are various ways in which the different aspects of this path can be grouped. One of the most basic is to divide it into the Path of Vision and the Path of Transformation.

The Path of Vision consists only of the stage of Perfect Vision. It begins when we catch a first glimpse of an entirely different way of being. The Path of Transformation comprises the other seven aspects of the Path and is the means by which we com-pletely reorient every facet of our being in such a way that it begins to accord with that initial vision.

THE PATH OF VISION
PERFECT VISION

The first glimmerings of Perfect Vision may arise spontaneously. Perhaps in a moment of inspiration we catch a glimpse of the vast inter-connectedness of all living things, or at a time of bereavement we see the futility of all our 'getting and spending'. Some catch their first glimpse of it through encountering another person and seeing a particular quality in the way they live their lives.

To the extent that they have any value at all, the great artistic, philosophical and religious productions of mankind embody some degree of Perfect Vision – to some extent at least, they all communicate something of how things really are.

Over the course of its two and half thousand year history Buddhism has generated a vast treasury of teachings – doctrines concerning the ultimate nature of reality and different methods for its realization. Fortunately, we don't have to master them all. All we need is what will help us to see more clearly how things really are and to act accordingly. One such teaching is that of the Three Marks of Conditioned Existence.

THE THREE MARKS OF CONDITIONED EXISTENCE

In his teaching, the Buddha distinguished between two different states – *samsara* and *nirvana*. *Samsara* pertains to the endless round of birth and death in which we find ourselves perpetually wandering. It is the state of un-Enlightened being. *Nirvana*, on the other hand, is that state of complete freedom and unending spontaneous creativity which follows from the complete eradication of craving.

The nature of *samsara* is that it is conditioned. How we are, what we think, what we feel, all arise in dependence upon conditions: our parents, schools, nation and race – all these have conditioned us in particular ways, and we continue to be conditioned by the news we read, the state of the weather, the food we eat and the company we keep. We have a reactive, coin-in-the slot kind of mentality. In goes an input, out comes an output. In goes sunshine, out comes happiness; in goes rain, out comes unhappiness.

Nirvana, on the other hand, which is synonymous with Enlightenment, is a state of complete, experiential insight into the conditioned nature of all phenomena. Seeing the conditioned nature of things, the Enlightened mind is not enslaved by them. The Enlightened mind is therefore completely creative – able to move in any direction at will, whatever it does will be free, fresh and spontaneous.

Conditioned existence has three marks or characteristics. It is unsatisfactory, impermanent, and insubstantial.

That conditioned existence is *unsatisfactory* was explained above under the heading of the First Noble Truth – the Truth of *dukkha*, unsatisfactoriness.

One of the main reasons why conditioned existence is unsatisfactory is because it is intrinsically *impermanent*. Nothing ever lasts. Whatever we want, whatever we get, slips in the end from our grasp. Everything, always, changes. How simple it is to say this, yet how difficult to truly realize it. We constantly treat conditioned phenomena as if they were permanent – our friends and family will always be around, our car will never break down, our favourite sweater will never wear out. Thus deluded, we experience *dukkha*.

Because conditioned things are intrinsically impermanent, they are also *insubstantial*. So far we've mainly concentrated on the psychological dimension of conditioned existence – nothing lasts and so we suffer. With the idea of insubstantiality we begin to enter the metaphysical dimension of conditionality.

Take, for example, the book you are now reading. It seems solid enough – just a normal book – but consider the conditions which went into making it. Think of the wood, which probably grew somewhere like Canada or Finland, which was chopped, pulped and turned into paper. Think of the sunshine that helped the trees grow, the woodsmen who tended them (and the food the woodsmen had to eat in order to function, the clothes they had to wear, the machinery they used). Think of the processes of transport involved at every stage. And then think of me, sitting here writing – my computer and printer – my food and clothing – my teacher, without whom I'd have nothing to say – my parents, without whom I would not exist – and all their parents, infinitely backwards in time.

Think of the publishers, the distributors, the booksellers. Think of the English language, all its vast history of development; and think also of Pali, Sanskrit, Tibetan, Chinese and Japanese. Think of the art of writing.

All of these are essential conditions which had to pre-exist in order for the book you're now reading to be what it is. If any of them were different, this book would not be what it is. In fact it wouldn't be here at all. For there is no essential 'book' which can somehow exist independently of all the myriad conditions which went into making it. All that it is is a temporary coming together of a vast range of conditions. And as conditions change, so it too changes – it wears out and grows grubby, or perhaps you'll get bored and throw it away. But whatever happens to it next, it never stops changing. Eventually it will be landfill, kindling or pulp for cardboard. There is nothing in it which you can hang on to and say 'This is it – this element here, that's the book!', because we could just throw it on a fire and it would vanish. There is no fixed, final, unchanging entity which is 'the book'.

We take the label 'the book' and apply it to a small temporary pattern within the infinite flux of conditions. We can use it with great accuracy for a time, to describe the particular way in which some conditions have come together. But that is all it is – a label – and we must never make the mistake of thinking that because we can use labels to denote patterns that there are somehow fixed and substantial, unchanging 'things' behind each label.

Because things are impermanent and insubstantial in this way, because they are only conditioned, they are also – to use an important Mahayana Buddhist concept – 'empty' or 'void'. All of phenomenal existence is *shunya*: empty. Things come together and pass away – there is no intrinsic reality behind them.

And yet, out of this changing flux of conditions, we construct for ourselves the delusion of solidity and intrinsic separation. We divide the world into subject and objects. There is 'me', a fixed, unchanging, solid ego-identity – and there is 'not me', the rest of life. And we then further divide the world into those things we like, which we seek to incorporate into our ego-identity to give us a sense of security; and those things which we dislike, which we try to keep apart from our ego-identity at all costs, because they make us insecure. This fundamental subject/object duality is the source of all our suffering.

Clinging to a changing world of flux, looking for security in the intrinsically insecure, we experience continual disappointment. The ultimate security we seek is not available in a dualized world founded in neurotic attachment. True security, rather, consists in learning to live without any neurotic attachments whatsoever. Such a state, however, is not one of sterile isolation from the rest of life. Rather, it is a state where we experience our deep inter-connectedness with *all* of life, where we don't try to shut some things or people out and grasp with clinging desperation to other things and people. We let things, people, ourselves, simply be what they really are – not what we want them to be. If we can just do that, then we will be free to respond to all living beings with kindness, warmth and compassion.

We must, however, beware of treating *samsara* and *nirvana* as entirely discrete opposites. For, as teachers like the great sage Nagarjuna have pointed out, they are in fact inseparable. It is not that *nirvana* is a place – as it were, a kind of Buddhist heaven, somewhere else – it is right here, right now.

To really see *samsara* as *samsara* is to experience *nirvana*. As Krishnamurti put it: 'The unconditional acceptance of the conditioned is the unconditioned.'

But we tend not to accept the conditioned as conditioned. We always want to treat it as if it were unconditioned, as if it were really able to give us complete and final satisfaction; as if the things we like and the people we love will somehow be with us forever; as if *samsara* were somehow really substantial and secure. And so we don't experience the identity of *samsara* and *nirvana*. We remain deluded. Misguidedly clinging to *samsara*, we suffer. We have a great deal of work to do before we ourselves can honestly say that we experience the identity of *samsara* and *nirvana*. For us *samsara* is here and *nirvana* is a state beyond the horizon of our current being, at the far end of a spiritual path which we can, if we chose, begin to tread.

To see the Three Marks of Conditioned Existence for ourselves – to realize their truth, not just intellectually but from the depths of our being, allowing our behaviour to be changed by that insight – is to have a meaningful glimpse of Perfect Vision and to take the first step along the Eightfold Path.

THE PATH OF TRANSFORMATION
PERFECT EMOTION

We can often see the truth of something quite clearly at an intellectual level, but we have deep emotional investments which keep us from acting on them. Most smokers, for example, know quite clearly that smoking is killing them and they should quit, but at a deeper, more emotional, less conscious level they have no intention whatever of stopping smoking. We are not moved by reason alone. Time and again we can see that the emotions are, in fact, stronger than reason, and if we want to do anything of any significance we can only do so with the full co-operation of the emotional side of our nature. For most of us, the central problem of the spiritual life is to find emotional equivalents for our intellectual understanding. For this reason, Perfect Emotion, *samma-samkalpa*, comes as the first step after Perfect Vision.

Samkalpa is often translated as 'resolve', or 'intention', or 'thought', but it is more like 'will'. It stands for the harmonization of the whole emotional and volitional side of our being with our vision of the true nature of existence.

Perhaps as a result of the theistic background of western culture, we tend to think, however unconsciously, that we are somehow fixed and unable to really change. 'I am as I am – take me or leave me.' Perhaps somewhere behind all this lurks the idea that 'I am as God made me and I can't do anything about it.' Buddhism, however, suggests that there is no divine plan. What we are now is the result of the conditions which have preceded us, and by changing some of the conditions in the present we can change ourselves for the future. In other words we can consciously set out to change our emotional state for the better.

The Buddhist tradition has evolved a vast range of practices which are intended to generate more positive mental and emotional states. I explain some of these in Chapter 5.

PERFECT SPEECH

In the west we tend to divide the individual human being into body and mind, or perhaps body, mind and soul. In Buddhism, however, the traditional division of a person is into body, *speech* and mind.

In all of nature, speech is the sole prerogative of human beings, and human culture depends upon it – through speech our mothers and teachers educated us, and almost all of our culture depends upon one or another form of vocal or textual expression. Speech gives shape to the world we live in. In naming things we colour them in a particular way, and in expressing our thoughts and feelings we make them part of the public domain we move in. What we express is a large part of who we are and how our world is.

It is very useful experience to keep silent for a few days – avoiding books, television and conversation – and to see what effect that has on your mental state. If conditions are right, as on some Buddhist retreats, most people find that sustained silence has a deeply clarifying and energizing effect.

But we are rarely silent. To live in the world is to speak, and because our speech has such a profound effect on us and on the world around us, it too must be transformed in the light of our glimpse of Perfect Vision. Perfect Speech, therefore, is speech which is first of all true.

> If you speak delusions, everything becomes a delusion;
> If you speak the truth, everything becomes the truth.
> Outside the truth there is no delusion,
> But outside delusion there is no special truth.
> Followers of the Buddha's Way!
> Why do you earnestly seek the truth in distant places?
> Look for delusion and truth in the bottom of your own hearts.[2]

To follow the Path indicated by our glimpse of Perfect Vision means to always uphold the truth in every situation, however uncomfortable that may be.

Perfect Speech also seeks to avoid creating unnecessary divisions between people – it is kindly, helpful and harmonious. Seeing the power of speech, moreover, and seeing how much energy can be frittered away through it, Perfect Speech is never merely frivolous (although it can be, and often is, light-hearted, ironic and humorous).

PERFECT ACTION

At the stage of Perfect Action, the glimpse of Perfect Vision begins to affect our lives by impinging directly on our behaviour. Perfect Action deals with the ethical dimension of life.

The western, Judaeo-Christian ethical system which we have inherited is generally conceived in terms of Law. Moral rules are laid upon humanity by God – as, for example, when Moses ascended Mount Sinai and brought down the tablets of stone which he then presented to the Children of Israel, in the midst of much awesome thunder and lightning.

As a result, we tend to treat ethics as if they were moral obligations being imposed upon us by a higher authority external to ourselves. Buddhist ethics, however, are not theological but psychological. Rather than 'good' or 'bad', Buddhism speaks of actions being 'skilful' or 'unskilful', and these are determined by the quality of the mental states which gave rise to them.

Perfect Vision reveals a world which is a constant flux of inter-connected conditions, where all living beings are interdependent. Skilful actions, motivated by generosity, kindness and understanding, accord with this vision of how things really are. They lead to a deepening of our experience of reality and a reduction of petty self-concern. Unskilful actions, motivated by greed, hatred and delusion, generate suffering and isolation, cut us off from the rest of life and reinforce the painful, constricting self-centredness from which they originated.

The Buddha never laid down a set of rules which all people

had to follow. He did, however, offer sets of ethical guidelines – patterns of behaviour which are a natural expression of skilful mental states. The most common of these is the set of the Five Precepts, which enjoin us to refrain from killing, stealing, sexual misconduct, lying and intoxication. I will describe these in more detail in Chapter 4.

PERFECT LIVELIHOOD

The preceding stages of the Noble Eightfold Path have all been concerned with how Perfect Vision transforms the individual human being. With Perfect Livelihood we are concerned with the transformation not only of the individual, but of society as well.

The world today is an increasingly large web of inter-connected activity, far more complex than it was in the Buddha's day. The indirect consequences of our day-to-day action are many and varied. For instance, by turning on a light we may be contributing to acid-rainfall on some distant forest through the sulphurous smoke from the power generating station; the exhaust gases released into the atmosphere from our using a car may play a part in the destruction of the ecology of sub-Saharan Africa; and by purchasing an ordinary white T-shirt we may be partly instrumental in polluting a river somewhere with bleach, and could quite probably be perpetuating a system of sweat-shop labour in the factory which made the shirt.

So long as we live in the modern industrialized world we are, almost from second to second, party to environmental destruction and economic exploitation.

At the same time, people in the industrialized nations are under tremendous pressure to produce and consume. Those who have work are wealthier than ever before, but they are under constant pressure to perform, and their leisure time is increasingly eroded. Alongside them, a smaller number of almost permanently unemployed people have large amounts of leisure time, but live in demeaning poverty. Neither of these options make it very easy to live a life dedicated to the unfolding of the implications of that first glimpse of Perfect Vision.

Recognizing the intrinsically unsatisfactory nature of getting and spending, Buddhists have always led simple lives – consuming little, sharing wherever possible, and gaining their livelihood in ways which support their spiritual endeavours. But in today's enormously complex world we cannot think of ourselves in isolation, whatever we do impinges on others and they on us. For this reason many Buddhists today see a need to work for social as well as personal change as part of their Buddhist practice. This is a theme I will return to in the concluding chapter.

PERFECT EFFORT

Bringing the whole of our lives around, so that they accord with the vision of existence revealed at the stage of Perfect Vision, is not an easy matter. We have such deeply ingrained habits. None the less, it is possible. All it takes is sustained effort.

The tradition offers another 'list' here – the Four Exertions. These consist of efforts to prevent the arising of unarisen unskilful mental states; to eradicate arisen unskilful mental states; to develop unarisen skilful mental states; and to maintain arisen skilful mental states.

1. Preventing the Arising of Unarisen Unskilful Mental States

There are six senses in the Buddhist scheme of things. The five senses that we are familiar with, together with the mind which is taken to be the sixth sense. Unskilful mental states arise when something enters the mind from memory, or one of the five senses, and we respond to that thing with craving or hatred. We see something attractive in a shop window as we are passing, and a craving begins – we want to have it, and that desire takes root in our minds and grows and strengthens until it is finally satisfied.

To prevent this from happening we have to 'guard the gates of the senses' and be vigilant about what we let in. By becoming more conscious of the sense impressions we let into our minds and of the thoughts, feelings and memories we entertain, we can begin to discriminate between inputs which lead to skilful mental states and those which don't.

2. Eradicating Arisen Unskilful Mental States

Another 'list' – there are five hindrances to spiritual progress: neurotic craving for sense experience (which leads to things like overeating); ill-will; sloth and torpor; restlessness and anxiety; and finally neurotic doubt and indecision (in the sense of not being able to commit oneself to the good). These are the fundamental unskilful mental states which we have to eradicate.

The mind which is free from these five hindrances is like a vast cool, clear lake. Neurotic craving, on the other hand, is like water which has had coloured dye added to it. At first it is all very colourful, very fascinating; we can be entranced by the way the colours swirl and mix, but in time the dyes mix together into a dull sludgy brown colour. Ill-will is like boiling water. Sloth and torpor is like a pond of water choked with weeds. Restlessness and anxiety is like a pond of water agitated by the wind. And neurotic doubt and indecision is just like mud.

In order to counteract these hindrances, the tradition offers four 'antidotes'. First, one considers the consequences of giving in to that mental state. If you allow yourself to get angry, you may speak harshly towards someone and cause them undue pain, or you may even become violent. What pain, chaos and confusion would result from that? Give in to greed and you just get fat. Is that what you wanted when you reached for the third slice of cake?

The second method is to cultivate the opposite. Every unskilful mental state has a skilful counterpart. If you feel aversion to someone, for example, you can work on cultivating feelings of kindness towards them. There are meditation practices designed to bring these kinds of changes about, and I describe one in particular in Chapter 5.

The third method is to allow the unskilful mental state to just pass by, without paying too much attention to it. Here, the mind is pictured like a clear blue sky, and passing mental states are just like clouds – they drift into the mind and drift out again. By not identifying with a passing mental state, by becoming bigger than it, we can sometimes allow it to simply pass away.

The fourth method, and one to be used only in the last resort, is simply suppression. This is not the same as 'repression', which is unconscious and psychologically harmful, but rather with full consciousness of what one is doing, one just grits one's teeth and refuses to succumb to the enticement of an unskilful mental state. This is how some people finally quit smoking, for example.

3. Developing Unarisen Skilful Mental States

One can develop skilful mental states via the enjoyment of nature or the arts, in communication with friends or through acts of kindness and generosity, but the principal method which Buddhists employ to develop skilful mental states is the systematic practice of meditation.

Buddhist meditation aims at the complete transformation of consciousness. It is a means whereby the mind works systematically and directly upon itself to bring about desired changes in the level of consciousness. Meditation has always been a central Buddhist practice – the Buddha gained Enlightenment during meditation. Buddhist iconography tends to centre on the subject, and all the great Buddhist masters have used it and taught it. There are thousands of Buddhist meditation techniques and I describe a representative sample of these in some detail in Chapter 5.

4. Maintaining Arisen Skilful Mental States

Having prevented and eradicated unskilful or negative mental states, and developed skilful or positive mental states, the essential thing is to keep on making the effort. It is very easy to slip back. Regular spiritual practice, of one sort or another, is the only way to keep ourselves making progress along the path. There comes a point when one has advanced so far along the path that further progress occurs naturally and spontaneously, but for the vast majority of us that point is a long way off. Until we reach it we are constantly subject to the gravitational pull of old habits and conditionings. Only regular practice – especially the practice of ethics, meditation and reflection on the Buddha's teachings – will keep us moving forward.

PERFECT AWARENESS

Our first glimpse of Perfect Vision was an instance of greater awareness, an awareness which is all too easily lost. At this stage of the path we are concerned with cultivating a higher and more continuous level of awareness.

The Pali word *sati*, which occurs at this stage of *samma-sati*, literally means something like 'recollection', but it is usually translated as 'mindfulness', or sometimes 'awareness'. The idea of mindfulness, or recollection, has connotations of continuity of purpose. Most of us are not particularly mindful or recollected in that sense. T.S. Eliot describes it well when he speaks of being 'distracted from distraction by distraction'.

The reason for this is that most of us are not one, unitary self but rather we're a loosely affiliated bundle of selves somehow getting by in the same body. Self number one, for example, may decide that she must definitely lose some weight this year. So she reads up on the latest diets and invests in a set of bathroom scales. Self number two, however, is having none of it. As soon as she gets the chance she's off to the refrigerator for another snack. Meanwhile, self number three is wondering whether perhaps a little infidelity isn't what's really called for to make life worth living. But self number four, which really took on board that strong Catholic conditioning, will only let that happen over their dead body! Which is probably just as well. What she really needs to make life worth living is to learn to meditate. That way all these different selves will get acquainted with one another, stop fighting and start moving in the same direction.

Not only are we psychologically fragmented, from the Buddhist point of view we are more often than not nearly asleep. Preoccupied with a confused whirl of fleeting sensations, memories, feelings, thoughts and emotions, we only have a very superficial awareness of the present moment. We're often simply lost in a haze of preoccupation and anxiety, or we're just numbed by the sheer sensory overload that comes from modern living – there are things to do, people to see, deadlines to meet. Very occasionally we may stop and look. Perhaps we're caught by the beauty of the sunset and we stop for a moment and pay attention to it. How different are those few moments of quiet, focused attention. A few moments of really being alive.

> Mindfulness is the Way to the Immortal, unmindfulness the way to death. Those who are mindful do not die, (whereas) the unmindful are like the dead.

> Knowing this distinction of mindfulness the spiritually mature rejoice in mindfulness and take delight in the sphere of the Noble Ones.

Absorbed in superconscious states, recollected, and ever
exerting themselves, those wise ones realize Nirvana, the
unsurpassed security.

Whosoever is energetic, recollected, pure in conduct,
considerate, self-restrained, of righteous life, and mindful, the
glory of such a one waxes exceedingly.

By means of energy, mindfulness, self-restraint and control,
let the man of understanding make (for himself) an island that no
flood can overwhelm.[3]

There are four principal objects in respect of which we can cultivate our awareness: ourselves, our environment, other people
and Reality.

We start with the body. It is worth stopping from time to time
and checking: how aware are you of your body, right now? Do
you know the position of your hands and feet? How is your
trunk and head? How exactly are you breathing? Are the
breaths short or long; deep or shallow? In order to develop and
maintain a continuous awareness of the body and its movements we have to slow down and learn to do only one thing at
a time. In that way we will not only begin to develop a more
continuous sense of ourselves, but our movements will become
more gracious and we will do whatever we set out to do more
effectively. Doing one thing at a time, with focused attention,
one can actually get far more done than if one rushes into activity in a continuous state of barely suppressed panic.

Next we come to the awareness of feelings and emotions.
There is a difference between them. Feelings are simple – they
are pleasant or painful, strong or weak. Emotions are generally
more complex. If we meet someone we like, we experience a
pleasant feeling, and then a whole mixed set of emotions aris-

es. Because our emotional lives are often quite convoluted, it's not always easy to become aware of emotions in all their depths and complexity. We can start by learning to recognize feelings as they arise – pleasant or painful – and by simply acknowledging our emotions as we become aware of them.

Some people in the west today tend to disown their emotions and repress them. Others are intensely preoccupied with all the subtle nuances of emotional life. Buddhism steers a middle way between these extremes. It simply suggests that we take our emotional state into account. Acknowledge it, and set about changing it – transforming negative emotions, developing and strengthening positive emotions.

Next we come to awareness of thoughts. Very often we don't know what we're thinking in any given moment. Thoughts just enter the mind at random, swirl about and then pass out again, having had very little meaningful effect. In becoming more aware of the process of thinking we make our thoughts more effective. By attending to the process of thinking, we can begin to follow individual thoughts through to their conclusion, and then act accordingly. Sustained, as opposed to discursive, thought is quite rare, but by bringing greater attention to our thinking processes we can begin to still the constant hum of discursive mental chatter and start to use our thoughts creatively. Eventually, through practices such as meditation, we can learn to still the chattering mind altogether for a time, leaving a pure, clear awareness and radiant consciousness.

Then there is awareness of the environment. As self-awareness deepens we also start to see the things outside of us with more clarity and to appreciate them with more depth – the motes of dust, dancing in a ray of light; the colours and textures of a bare brick wall; birdsong; the colours of autumn leaves.

We also start to attend more closely to other people, to sense their feelings and emotions as they show them in their posture and expression, and to attend to them more closely. It is rare these days to be really listened to. Sometimes the greatest gift we can give someone is just to hear them out, with our full, undivided attention.

Finally we come to the highest level of awareness of all. The awareness of Reality. To start with, we need to recognize that generally speaking we are *not* aware of Reality. We spend much of the time in a world of delusive projection, taking our immediate, subjective responses to things and treating them as if they were ultimately real and had an existence apart from ourselves. Projecting them on to reality, we live in worlds built from the thin fabric of our desires and aversions. When we are down, the world really *is* a grim pit of despair; when we are happy it's a cheerful pleasure park. In order to become more aware of how things really are, we can begin by being less attached to our immediate subjective responses to things – trying to be more objective in our assessments.

We can also reflect more deeply on those truths which were revealed in our first glimpse of Perfect Vision, turning them over in our mind, trying to keep them present to us, allowing them to transform us at deeper and deeper levels. And we can contemplate formulations which point out the true nature of things. Formulas such as the Four Noble Truths or the Three Marks of Conditioned Existence.

PERFECT SAMADHI

The word *samadhi* literally means the state of being fixed, or established. This can be understood in two ways. It can represent the fixation of the mind on a single object, as in meditative concentration, or it can represent the state of being fixed or established in Ultimate Reality. Used in this latter way, Perfect *Samadhi* represents the culmination of the Path, the point at which one's initial vision has been realized in full and one's whole being has been utterly and irreversibly transformed.

Traditionally, there are three *samadhis* in this higher sense of the term. Although far beyond most of us, they are worth dwelling on to some extent, as they give us a taste of the goal. These are not mutually exclusive states, rather they represent different dimensions of the one *samadhi*.

First there is the Imageless *Samadhi*. This indicates the freedom of the state of *samadhi* from all conceptualization. It is a state of complete consciousness, fully aware at the very highest level, but without a single discursive thought. Like a luminous, clear blue sky, without even a hint of cloud.

Then there is the Directionless *Samadhi*, a state of being completely at rest, with no impulse to move in any direction. It is completely poised, like a perfect sphere, resting on a perfect plane. It can move anywhere but there is no impulse to move. All egotistic desire has been eliminated. It is a state of perfect spontaneity, but with no impulse to do anything.

Finally, there is the *Samadhi* of Emptiness. This is a state of complete realization of the Ultimate Nature of Reality – that all things whatsoever have the same nature, and that nature is no-nature. As we read in the *Heart Sutra*:

... form is no other emptiness
Emptiness no other than form
Form is only emptiness
Emptiness only form
Feeling, thought and choice
Consciousness itself
Are the same as this.

All things are the primal void,
Which is not born or destroyed.

Nor is it stained or pure,
Nor does it wax or wane ...

... So know that the Bodhisattva,
Holding to nothing whatever
But dwelling in prajna wisdom,
Is freed of delusive hindrance
Rid of the fear bred by it
And reaches clearest Nirvana.

All Buddhas of past and present,
Buddhas of future time,
Using this prajna wisdom,
Come to full and perfect vision ...[4]

The Eightfold Path concludes here – or rather at this point it disappears altogether from sight, running on, far beyond the horizon of our current consciousness, into dimensions of ever higher freedom and creativity.

But we must beware of thinking of the Eightfold Path as somehow having a discrete beginning, middle and end, as if each stage were to be traversed once and once only. Rather, the path is cumulative. With each step along the Path of Transformation our capacity for Perfect Vision deepens. The stronger our vision, the more impelled we will be to work on transforming ourselves. Sometimes we make slow, steady progress, at other times we can have quite dramatic break-throughs. Sometimes we may even feel stuck. But as long as we keep on making the effort, progress is eventually assured.

These teachings – the Four Noble Truths; the Noble Eightfold Path; the Three Marks of Conditioned Existence; the Intrinsic Emptiness of all Phenomena; the Identity of *Samsara* and *Nirvana*; the Five Precepts; meditation; the Four Exertions; the

Five Hindrances; the Four Antidotes; the Four Objects of Awareness; the Three *Samadhis* – contain within them a life-time's worth of practise. Although only a tiny fraction of the Buddhist teachings, they may give us some sense at least of what the Dharma is all about.

References

1) Sangharakshita, *Vision and Transformation* (Windhorse Publications, 1990)

2) transl. Stevens, John. *One Robe, One Bowl: The Zen Poetry of Ryokan* (Weatherhill, 1984)

3) From the *Dhammapada* – section on Mindfulness, verses 21–25, transl. Sangharakshita (unpublished)

4) transl. Kapleau, Philip. The Heart Sutra from *The FWBO Puja Book: A Book of Buddhist Devotional Texts* (Windhorse Publications, 1984)

THE SANGHA

When the Buddha 'went forth' from home to become a wandering mendicant, he was following a practice fairly common at the time. Others, too, roamed the countryside, singly or in bands, under the leadership of a spiritual teacher or alone. And in gathering his first disciples together in the deer-park at Sarnath, the Buddha was simply doing what other spiritual teachers of the time did, for the broad community of wandering ascetics was already divided into a number of *sanghas* – religious fellowships – centred on particular teachers. Like Mahavira, the founder of the Jains, the Buddha would have appeared to others at the time to be simply another founder and head of one such *sangha*. Like the others, he taught a particular *dharma*, and it was this, rather than their way of life, which distinguished his followers from the rest.

The Buddha and his first disciples lived a life based on the unwritten code of the broader ascetic community. They wore robes made of cast-off rags, shaved off their hair and spent most of the year roaming from place to place. They lived on alms; abstained from sexual intercourse; from theft; from killing and from making false claims about their spiritual attainments. Like members of other wandering sects, they held fortnightly meetings at which they recited a *pratimoksha* (Pali *patimokkha*), or verse summary of the special Dharma to which they adhered.

One such verse summary has been preserved in the *Dhammapada*:

> Abstention from all evil,
> Cultivation of the wholesome,
> Purification of the Heart:
> This is the Message of the Buddhas.

> Forbearance is the highest ascetic practice;
> 'Nirvana is supreme', say the Buddhas.
> He is not 'gone forth' who harms another;
> He is not a recluse who molests another.

> Not to speak ill, not to injure,
> To observe the patimokkha,
> To be moderate in eating,
> To live alone in a secluded abode,
> To devote oneself to meditation:
> This is the Message of the Buddhas.[1]

The word *sangha* has many meanings. Italicized, we use it in the most general Pali or Sanskrit sense to mean simply a group or collection of people. In this sense it has passed into the modern Indian languages. Capitalized, however, we use it in one or another particularly Buddhist sense. As the third of the Three Jewels – the Buddha, the Dharma and the Sangha – it refers exclusively to the *Arya* Sangha, the Noble Sangha: all those whose spiritual attainments are such that there is no possibility of their ever falling back into the grip of *samsara*.

More generally, Sangha is also used to refer to the wider

Buddhist spiritual community – all those who follow the Buddha's teachings and live according to his Dharma.

GOING FOR REFUGE

As the Buddha wandered from place to place he encountered people, got into conversation with them, and very often his words would have a tremendous impact on them. They would speak of light having been brought where there was previously darkness, of something which had been overturned being set upright again. And sometimes the effect on them of hearing the Dharma for the first time was so dramatic that it completely reoriented their entire lives, changed the way they saw themselves and the world, and had profound implications for how they were going to live in the future. And they would express this fact in these words:

Buddham saranam gacchami!
Dhammam saranam gacchami!
Sangham saranam gacchami!

To the Buddha for Refuge I Go!
To the Dharma for Refuge I Go!
To the Sangha for Refuge I Go!

In other words, they committed themselves to completely reorienting their lives around the Three Jewels. They took the Buddha as their teacher and his Enlightenment as their ultimate goal; they took his Dharma as their guide; and they aspired to membership (or in some cases even proclaimed their membership) of the Arya Sangha and sought its assistance in their endeavours.

This act of Going for Refuge to the Three Jewels is what

makes one a Buddhist. And, no matter how much they have diverged over the centuries, it remains common to all schools of Buddhism.

The word 'refuge' can be misleading at first. Some people read it as 'escape', as if Buddhism were a form of escapism. But, in fact, the very opposite is true. The act of taking refuge in something is not confined to Buddhism. It is endemic to the human condition. When we go for refuge to something, we put that thing in the centre of our lives and we try to organize our lives around it – we use it to give sense and meaning to our lives. And we go for refuge to all sorts of different things.

Some people go for refuge to their careers. Defining them-selves in terms of their job – 'I am a schoolteacher, or I am a lawyer, or I am a builder' – they gain a sense of security in the face of the chaos of ordinary life. They know who they are and where they stand. Or we take refuge in a lover, a husband or wife. We believe that these at least will always be reliable sources of support and comfort. People also take refuge in the things they own – their car may be a central part of their iden-tity: the exact model and colour they choose proclaims just where they stand in the overall scheme of things.

But none of these refuges is ultimately secure. Everything mundane is subject to change. We can always lose our job. Our loved ones may cease to love us. Our car may be stolen or dam-aged – eventually, like everything else, it will just fall apart. This is not to say that we have to abandon our careers, loved ones and possessions in order to live a spiritual life (although some do). It is simply to point out the inevitable insecurity of organizing one's whole life around things which are condi-tioned and therefore subject to change. The only secure refuge is Enlightenment – the Unconditioned. Placing the goal of Enlightenment in the centre of one's life, one can then organize all the other elements of one's life around it.

The way in which placing the Three Jewels at the centre of one's life will affect the other elements within it depends upon the extent to which one Goes for Refuge, for not all Buddhists Go for Refuge to the same extent. There are four principal levels of Going for Refuge:

First there is the 'Ethnic' level of Going for Refuge. This is the level of people who consider themselves to be Buddhists because they were born into a Buddhist family or live in a Buddhist country (if, indeed, a country can be said to be Buddhist). Such a person carries out his or her religious duties in a nominal fashion because they are what is expected of someone living in that society. They simply do their duties as members of the group to which they belong. They call themselves Buddhist, but it is no more than a mark of cultural belonging or group allegiance.

The Ethnic level is well and good so far as it goes, but in itself it doesn't go very far. It will not have a very significant transforming effect on the lives of those whose practice remains only at that level. For Buddhism to have a meaningful impact on our lives it must be consciously undertaken. One cannot be born on to the spiritual path.

Second, there is 'Provisional' Going for Refuge. People at this level have different degrees of experience of the path. They may be attending their first Buddhist meditation class, or trying, for the first time, to live by Buddhist ethical principles, or they may have been applying Buddhist doctrines and methods to their lives for many years but are not yet ready to finally commit themselves to the Three Jewels. Anyone who wishes to know what Buddhism is all about can only do so by passing through this level. Buddhism is *ehipassiko* – a Pali word for 'come and see'. It can only be understood through direct, personal experience.

Third, there is 'Effective' Going for Refuge. This is the level of people who have committed themselves to the Three Jewels – who have put the Three Jewels into the centre of their lives and oriented the rest of their activities around them. They make an effort to create conditions which will support their own and others' practice of Buddhism, and, so long as the prevailing conditions support it, their practice of Buddhism remains effective. They may live as monks or householders; alone or in a residential spiritual community. They keep up a regular meditation practice; study the Dharma; maintain close contact with other members of the Sangha and apply Buddhist ethical principles to all their activity.

Finally there is 'Real' Going for Refuge. This is the level of those Buddhist practitioners who have, to some extent, broken free of the gravitational pull of *samsara*. Through continuous spiritual effort, leading to the arising of spiritual insight, they have achieved a level of spiritual creativity which is irreversible. No longer confined by the limits of mundane personality, they have unshakeable faith in the Three Jewels; their ethical practice is impeccable; and their lives are naturally dedicated to liberation, without distinction of self or other.

Beings at this highly advanced level of practice are said to have 'Entered the Stream', or manifested the Will to Enlightenment. The traditional texts delineate a number of states of further development through which they can still pass, but these members of the Noble Sangha already live their lives at a level far beyond any which most of us can discern – *'Like birds in the sky, those trackless ones, how can you trace them?'*

THE GROWTH AND DEVELOPMENT OF THE SANGHA

Although the Buddha's first disciples were wandering mendicants like himself, householders too soon wanted to join his growing Sangha. Not all of these 'went forth' into homeless life, but many made considerable spiritual progress – the Pali scriptures, for example, record the names of 21 fully Enlightened householders and many dozens who achieved at least Stream Entry.

In time there arose a fourfold division within the Sangha: monks, nuns (*bhikkhus, bhikkhunis*), laymen and laywomen. But it was still seen to be one Sangha, although its members might choose different lifestyles.

> Brethren, these four persons, who are full of wisdom and insight, are well-disciplined, learned [in the Dharma] and have reached complete righteousness, shed lustre upon the Sangha. Which are the four? Brethren, the monk, the nun, the male lay devotee, the female lay devotee, who are full of wisdom and insight, well-disciplined, and learned, and have reached complete righteousness, shed lustre upon the Sangha. Brethren, these four beings do indeed shed lustre upon the Sangha.[2]

At first, monastic ordination into the Buddha's growing spiritual community was very simple. Someone would proclaim their intention to Go for Refuge to the Three Jewels, and the Buddha would simply reply 'Come, *bhikkhu*, live the spiritual life for the utter cessation of suffering.' And the person who was thus addressed 'went forth' and became a member of the *bhikkhu* Sangha.

But some time after the Buddha's death things began to change. The community of homeless wanderers began to settle down in monasteries. The simple *pratimoksha* evolved into a detailed code of monastic discipline which in time developed into a vast and somewhat legalistic body of work. Comprising six substantial volumes in the English translation, it governs with minute attention all the details of how monastic life should be lived. Different branches of the monastic order follow different (though very similar) sets of rules, but there came to be at least 227 rules for the monks and 311 for the nuns.

Being full-timers in the spiritual life, religious professionals, as it were, the monastic order preserved and transmitted the Dharma. And, quite naturally, the teachings which they preserved and transmitted tended to be those which were of most interest to themselves. In time the word Sangha came to be appropriated by the monastic order to itself alone, and thus today, in some parts of the Buddhist world, the word 'Sangha', in all its uses, is taken to mean exclusively the order of monks – the *bhikkhu* Sangha (the order of nuns having died out in places where this is the case.)

This rigidity on the part of some elements within the early monastic order led, about 140 years after the Buddha's death, to the first major schism in the order. On the one side were the Sthaviravadins, or 'School of the Elders' (i.e. the senior monks), according to whom Buddhism was primarily, if not exclusively, a religion for monks. They alone had the right of determining what was Buddhism and what was not, and they sought to impose their version of the Buddha's teaching on the entire Buddhist community. On the other side were the Mahasanghikas, 'Those of the Great Order'. They were the liberal party, representing all four divisions of the Sangha – monks, nuns, laymen and laywomen. They maintained that because the Dharma had been taught for the benefit of all, irrespective of socio-ecclesiastical status, the right of determining the true nature of the teachings lay with the whole Buddhist community, not with any one section of it exclusively, and in compiling a standard version of the Buddha's teaching all surviving traditions should be taken into account, including those current among the laity.

They also felt that there should be a common spiritual ideal, not a higher one for monks and nuns and a lower one for lay people. As the Mahasanghikas were, by all accounts, the larger party, they probably represented contemporary Buddhist thought more faithfully than the Sthaviravadins, who consisted only of some of the senior members belonging to a particular group of monasteries.

Out of the Sthaviravada arose a succession of schools afterwards known collectively to their opponents as the Hinayana or 'Little Way' and from the Mahasanghikas there sprang up various schools which gave rise to a movement calling itself the Mahayana, or 'Great Way', which sought to restate the Buddha's teachings in terms more in keeping with its original spirit.

Driven by the universalism and optimism that had given it birth, the Mahayana evolved for all followers of the Buddha a common spiritual ideal which derived inspiration as much from the living personal example of the Buddha as from the records of his teaching. This was the ideal of the *Bodhisattva* – one whose heart is set upon Enlightenment for the sake of living beings. At the same time it worked out a common path for monks and laity alike – the Path of the *Paramitas* or 'Perfections', the most common of which is a list of Six. The Mahayana sought to overcome the spiritual individualism which had infected the Sangha by stressing the ideal of working for the good, not only of oneself, but all living beings. The Six Perfections, by means of which the aspiring Bodhisattva trains to this end are Perfect Generosity, Ethics, Patience, Vigour, Meditation and Wisdom.

By stressing the fact that all, whether monks or laymen, could be Bodhisattvas, and thus potential Buddhas, the Mahayana was able to lessen the tensions between the divisions of the Sangha, which were now united through the pursuit of a common spiritual objective and the practice of the same, or similar, spiritual methods. Some Mahayanists lived as monks, following a monastic code not dissimilar to that of the conservative Sthaviravadins and their various successors; others lived as householders.

Today the Sthaviravadins live on only in the form of Theravada Buddhism, which predominates throughout southeast Asia, whilst the various forms of Tibetan and Sino-Japanese Buddhism are off-shoots of the Mahayana.

From this point onwards the more colourful and dramatic developments in Buddhism all took place within the context of the Mahayana, the so-called Hinayana schools getting on primarily with the business of preserving the Buddha's basic teachings (for which task all Buddhists should be deeply grateful); developing the Abhidharma, a work of monumental intellectual achievement; and elaborating on the Vinaya – the monastic code.

UNFOLDING THE RICHES OF THE ARYA SANGHA

With the development of the Mahayana, the *Arya* Sangha was enriched by the figure of the Bodhisattva, human and even supra-human beings whose lives were dedicated to the pursuit of Enlightenment, not for themselves alone but for all living beings.

As the figure of the human, historical, Buddha receded in time, the focus of people's devotions shifted from the person of the Buddha to the ideal of Buddhahood itself. Buddhahood, in turn, was seen to have various different aspects, such as Wisdom and Compassion. Contemplated with the eye of the spiritual imagination, these different aspects in turn came to be represented as separate personifications of Buddhahood, appearing as transcendental Buddha figures – shimmering, incandescent forms, made entirely of light, emanating from the Void and radiating their particular quality in all directions of space and time. Thus, for example, Compassion came to be seen in the form of the Buddha Amitabha, the Buddha of Eternal Light, who is made entirely of warm red light, glowing like the setting sun.

In time a total of five Buddhas appeared. They manifested as a *mandala*, a schematic arrangement, and, as the different qualities of Buddhahood came to be seen in more detail, each of the different Buddhas developed a spiritual family – the transcendental Bodhisattvas: sons and daughters of the Buddhas, lighting up the spiritual firmament with the blazing qualities of their compassionate action for the sake of all living beings.

The most popular of these transcendental Bodhisattva figures is Avalokiteshvara, son of the Buddha Amitabha, and the archetype of Universal Compassion. Avalokiteshvara, appearing in the form of a young Indian prince, richly adorned, made entirely of bright white light, sitting in meditation posture and with four arms, represents the activity of Enlightened Compassion in the world. Like the other figures in the *mandala*, Avalokiteshvara came to be associated with a particular *mantra*. Just as the figures themselves are symbols made of light, so the *mantras* are symbols made of sound. Avalokiteshvara's *mantra* – OM MANI PADME HUM – became enormously popular throughout the Indo-Tibetan Buddhist world as an evocation of the qualities of Enlightened Compassion.

In Tibet Avalokiteshvara is known and revered as Chenresig, and his *mantra* is carved or painted on rocks and stones throughout the land. As Buddhism spread to China Avalokiteshvara changed sex and became the benign and elegant white-robed Kuan Yin – the female Bodhisattva of Compassion. In Japan, Kuan Yin is known as Kannon or Kanzeon. All these changes of form are most fitting for a

Bodhisattva whose particular quality is to appear to beings in whatever form is most suited to their needs.

Perhaps 1000 years after the Buddha's death, particularly in north-western India and Nepal, the Mahayana began to develop into Tantric, or Vajrayana Buddhism. The Vajrayana, or Diamond Way, transmuted the spirits, sprites, fiends and demons which haunted the popular imagination, 'converting' them to Buddhism, incorporating them into the Five Buddha *mandala*, thus further enriching the *Arya* Sangha.

FURTHER DEVELOPMENTS IN THE SANGHA

As Zen Buddhism came to prominence in Japan from around the thirteenth century, the *Arya* Sangha was enriched by the figure of the *roshi*: one who has experienced the chief aim of that tradition – direct penetrative insight into the true nature of reality. Technically speaking, a *roshi* is therefore at least a Stream Entrant. Whether this is true of all those who bear the title today, however, is not altogether clear.

In Tibet, around the same time, the *tulku* system began to develop. *Tulkus* are *bodhisattvas*, either human or supra-human, incarnated in human form for the sake of leading human beings to liberation. These are the so-called reincarnate *lamas* (*lama* is the Tibetan equivalent of the Sanskrit term *guru*, or teacher). The *tulku* system, which is closely bound up with the Tibetan feudal system, superseded both the *bodhisattva* and the monastic ordination, with the *tulkus* becoming the chief teachers and the sources of all spiritual (and often mundane) authority. *Tulkus* are often known by the title *rimpoche* – greatly precious one. Some *tulkus* live as ordained monks, others marry and live as householders. Whatever their chosen lifestyle, they are all deeply respected and revered by Tibetan Buddhists.

Technically speaking, all *tulkus* are incarnated *bodhisattvas*. That this is true of all those who claim to be *tulkus* today, however, is not something that one can unequivocally assert.

In the nineteenth century, the new Meiji government in Japan decreed that all monks should marry. *Bodhisattva* ordination began to replace monastic ordination, but as this was granted only to those directly involved in pastoral activity, it lost the unifying effect it had displayed in earlier times and became, in many quarters, simply a mark of religious professionalism.

As Buddhism has come to the west, so too have all these different manifestations of the Buddhist Sangha. One can meet Tibetan *tulkus* and *bhikshus*; Japanese and American *roshis*; Thai, Burmese, Sri Lankan and British *bhikkhus*. And, as Buddhism begins to take root in the west, new western models of Sangha are evolving in direct response to the particular conditions which prevail here today.

WOMEN IN BUDDHISM

Taken as a whole, the Buddhist scriptures are ambiguous concerning the place of women in Buddhism. On the one hand the Buddha was unequivocal about the fact that women, as much as men, could gain Enlightenment, and he admitted them into the monastic order, ordaining them as *bhikkhunis* – a development which was utterly revolutionary at the time. On the other hand, we are told that he was very reluctant to do so, and only gave way after being begged three times to do so by Ananda. Moreover, when he did finally admit them he gave them a set of precepts which include but exceed all of those followed by their monastic brothers.

In the Mahayana scriptures there are a number of instances where the inferior nature of birth as a woman is asserted, whilst on the other hand, in the very same body of literature, there are ironic stories of young women chiding, and finally discomfiting, venerable old monks for not recognizing women's abilities to master the teachings.

The full *bhikkhuni* ordination lineage died out in the Theravada. It was never successfully exported to Tibet and today it survives only in the Chinese traditions. There are women living a monastic life as *anis* amongst the Tibetan community or as *maejis* in Thailand, but their 'status' is seen to be considerably inferior to that of the 'fully ordained' monks who live (outwardly at least) according to the old established monastic codes, and the facilities they enjoy are meagre, to say the least.

Amongst Buddhist practitioners in the west, however, the picture is very different, with the vast majority of Buddhist organizations admitting women and men on a completely equal basis.

There is a move on the part of some women in the west, and increasingly in the east, to find ways of reviving the traditional *bhikshuni*[3] ordinations – perhaps by 'importing' into Theravada or Tibetan Buddhism the existing Chinese ordination lineage, which is said to go back in an unbroken line all the way to the first women's ordinations at the time of the Buddha. Whether or not these actually do so it is impossible finally to know, but in any event the women who wish to revive such ordination find themselves in a cleft stick. On the one hand they seek equality with their monastic brothers. To do so they wish to revive the traditional *bhikshuni* ordination. But the traditional *bhikshuni* ordination thus revived would unequivocally place them on a footing inferior to that of the monks. One of the rules which they would have to take, for example, asserts that any nun, 'even of 100 years seniority' must defer at all times to the very youngest monk!

It would seem that those women who genuinely seek equality of opportunity and ordination in the Buddhist context would do best by putting aside the whole question of *bhikshuni* ordination and taking up one of the new models of ordination and practice which are coming into being in the west today, where men and women take the same ordination and have the same opportunities for practice.

SPIRITUAL FRIENDSHIP

Although periods of solitude may be helpful from time to time, Buddhism cannot ultimately be practised in complete isolation. If, however provisionally, one Goes for Refuge to the Three Jewels, one needs the support of others.

A Sangha, or spiritual community, is made up of men and women who share a common ideal: they all go for refuge to the Three Jewels. They have come together out of a mutual concern to pursue the goal of Enlightenment – to cultivate skilful mental states and to reduce unskilful mental states. Holding their highest ideals in common, they are able to form spiritual friendships with one another. Spiritual friendship, *kalyana mitrata*, is a friendship (*mitrata*) which is wholesome, beautiful, or noble (*kalyana*).

There are two kinds of spiritual friendship. 'Horizontal' spiritual friendship, which pertains to people at more or less the same level of spiritual attainment, and 'vertical' spiritual friendship, which takes place between people at different stages of the path. One needs spiritual guides and one needs friends – companions who share in one's struggles and achievements.

As we have seen, the Buddha himself always went on his wanderings with a close companion. Much of the time he was accompanied by his friend and cousin Ananda. One day Ananda, who had been thinking deeply about things for a while, turned to the Buddha and exclaimed:

> Lord, I've been thinking – spiritual friendship is at least half of
> the spiritual life!

The Buddha replied:

> Say not so, Ananda, say not so. Spiritual friendship is the whole
> of the spiritual life![4]

There are many reasons for this. First, one has to learn the path
to Enlightenment in large part from others. This is how the
Dharma has been preserved for the last two and a half thousand years – teachers have passed their knowledge and experience on to their disciples in an unbroken chain of spiritual
friendship which reaches back to the Buddha himself. Without
those friendships the path to Enlightenment would have van-
ished into the mists of time.

Spiritual friendship also provides a context for self-transcendence, giving one an opportunity to put another's needs
beyond one's own. It's easy to say that our sense of ourselves is
ultimately illusory, and therefore we should care for others as
much as ourselves. Practising that is very much harder. But in
a strong spiritual friendship it's much easier to put at least *one*
person's needs above our own. That would be a very good
start.

The Buddha once went to visit his cousin, the monk
Anuruddha, and his two friends, who were living together at
the 'Eastern Bamboo Park':

> 'I hope that you all live in concord, as friendly and undisputing
> as milk with water, viewing each other with kindly eyes.'

'That we certainly do,' Anuruddha replied. 'It is gain and good fortune for me to be living with such spiritual friends. I maintain acts, words and thoughts of loving-kindness towards them, both in public and in private. I think "Why should I not set aside what I am minded to do and do only what they are minded to do?" and I act accordingly. We are different in body, but only one in mind, I think.'[5]

There is also the question of openness and communication. Many people have a private side to their lives which they are unwilling to disclose to others. They may be ashamed of certain aspects of their behaviour – irrationally or with good reason – or there may be parts of themselves which they can't express because they hardly understand them themselves. In communication between friends these shadowy parts of the psyche become clearer and we come to a deeper understanding of ourselves. This is an important part of the process of letting go of a fixed sense of selfhood, but it can be very difficult to simply let go in the company of strangers, or those who don't share one's ideals.

It is also very easy to fool oneself in the context of spiritual practice – to let things slip and pretend to oneself that one's little (or even big) transgressions don't really matter. But when ideals are held in common they're more easily kept alive. When one falls back, a friend can lend a hand with encouragement or admonition.

The atmosphere of warmth and trust, so necessary to the functioning of any spiritual community, can only come about where there are deep, effective spiritual friendships present. This is something we especially need to develop in modern western society, which is so marked by states of alienation, loneliness and isolation.

The cultivation of effective spiritual friendships is a vital part of Buddhist practice. Without them, the ideal of Sangha never becomes more than that – an ideal.

References

1) From the *Dhammapada* , verses 184–6, quoted in Sangharakshita, *The Three Jewels*, Windhorse Publications, 1991.

2) *Anguttara-Nikaya* II–1-vii.

3) *Bhikshuni* is Sanskrit, *bhikkuni* is Pali, they both mean 'nun'.

4) *Samyutta-Nikaya*, verse 2.

5) Bhikkhu Nanamoli. *The Life of the Buddha* , Buddhist Publication Society, 1984.

BUDDHIST ETHICS

KARMA

As I have explained, the fundamental Buddhist teaching is the doctrine of conditionality. Everything arises in dependence upon conditions, nothing has a fixed and final essence – and this includes ourselves. What we are now is the result of the conditions of our past, what we become in the future will be determined by the conditions of the present, and one of the chief determining factors in what we become in the future is how we behave now. As we do, so we become. This fact, the Buddha saw, is what makes the spiritual life possible. By beginning to change our behaviour we begin to make ourselves differently. This is the root of all creativity – we are not doomed to simply repeating past patterns of behaviour, endlessly re-becoming the same old person, again and again. We can make ourselves anew. Every moment of life presents an endless array of possibilities.

How we make ourselves, what we become, is determined by the quality of our *karma* – our volitional actions. Often misunderstood as a form of universal divine retribution, the Buddhist Law of *karma* simply proposes that our volitional actions inevitably have consequences for us. It is just an extension of the more fundamental doctrine of conditionality.

According to the *Atthasalini*, one of the earlier commentaries, there are five distinct orders of conditionality, five *niyamas*, an examination of which will throw some light on to the Buddhist idea of *karma*.

The first and most fundamental order of conditionality is the 'physical inorganic'. Under this category we find all the laws which determine the way in which matter functions at the inorganic level. This order encompasses all the laws of physics and chemistry.

The next, slightly higher level, is the 'physical organic', which encompasses all the laws of the biological sciences.

Then there is the 'psychological' level. Here are found all the laws which govern the involuntary, instinctive operations of the mind. That our hand recoils after touching a hot coal, for example, is an instance of the operation of this order of conditionality.

Next comes the *karmic* level, which comprises all the laws which govern the way in which volitional activity affects consciousness.

And finally there is the *Dharmic* level. This describes what we might call 'transcendental' conditionality – a level of conditionality which is experienced chiefly by members of the *Arya* Sangha. Since this level of conditionality only affects us to the extent that we interact with such illustrious beings, and even then we will be unable to perceive it, we will say no more about it.

The first three levels of conditionality – physical inorganic, physical organic and psychological – are familiar to us from our days in school laboratories, making explosions, racing rats through mazes or whatever. We in the west today have penetrated more deeply into these areas of knowledge than any other people in history. But we only have a very rudimentary, even primitive, awareness of the *karmic*, or ethical dimension of life. Buddhism, on the other hand, is founded, perhaps above all, on an understanding of the operation of the *karmic* dimension of conditionality, for it is the fact that we can change the patterns of behaviour which result in our being bound up in *samsara* which lies at the very heart of Buddhism.

The fact that our behaviour conditions our being is the essence of Buddhist ethics. But it is not just *what* we do that matters. What is crucial is the state of mind from which we act.

Buddhist ethics is an ethics of intention. Acts themselves are neutral, what matters is the mental state, the volition behind the act. Buddhism doesn't speak in terms of right or wrong, good or bad. Instead it speaks in terms of skilful or unskilful intentions. Skilful volitions, founded in generosity, love and clarity, have karmically positive outcomes: they lead one away from delusion and towards Enlightenment. Unskilful volitions, founded in greed, hatred and spiritual ignorance, are what keep us circling in *samsara* in an endless round of repetitive, habitual attachment.

Buddhism distinguishes between 'natural morality' and 'conventional morality'. Conventional morality is simply the set of rules and customs according to which any group operates. It will vary from place to place and time to time – some cultures practise polygamy, whilst in others it is abhorrent. Christians happily eat pork, but Muslims and Jews find that repugnant. Conventional morality may have arisen in response to particular social circumstances, but it has a way of lingering after the event. For example, there are no longer valid hygienic grounds to abhor the eating of pork, but you still can't buy it in Jeddha or Jerusalem.

Natural morality is based on the facts of human psychology and the operation of the Law of Karma. In natural morality, acts are judged to be skilful or unskilful, not depending on the views or customs of the group, but depending on whether or not they have spiritually beneficial outcomes. Skilful actions lead one out of *samsara*, they bring about greater expansiveness, clarity and happiness: less egocentricity. Unskilful actions reinforce the ego-sense: they lead to constriction and attachment and bind us to *samsara*. In short, acts may be judged skilful or unskilful depending on whether or not they lead us towards, or away from, Enlightenment.

REBIRTH

Buddhism teaches that we don't always experience the results of our karma immediately – they may come to fruition much later, even in future lives. Buddhists throughout the ages have taught that the process of re-becoming applies not only to this life, where we make ourselves anew from moment to moment, but that even beyond the apparent barrier of death our habitual volitions determine the manner in which we are re-born.

Rebirth in this sense is not the same as reincarnation. It is not that a fixed, unchanging spiritual essence finds itself a new home in another body once the previous one has worn out. Rather, the continuum of change simply runs along, in much the way that a flame moves through a dry bunch of twigs, passing from one twig to the next. One cannot say that it is the same flame which burns in every twig. The flame never stops changing, and in a similar way it is not the same 'self' that is reborn.

Some western Buddhists find the idea of rebirth hard to take and have argued that, given the lack of empirical evidence, we must necessarily remain agnostic on this issue. Others argue that, although scant, there is *some* evidence, empirical or otherwise, to support the case for rebirth.[1] They point to a variety of scientific studies of the issue; instances of hypnotic regression; the involuntary recollection of details about past lives;

near-death experiences; and the case of child prodigies, such as Mozart, who played and composed music at the age of four. Some also maintain that there is more evidence (albeit slight) for a continuation of consciousness after death than there is for its cessation which, by definition, is not a theory amenable to empirical determination.

But, whatever we may think in the west today, for the last two and a half thousand years no major Buddhist teacher, however iconoclastic, has questioned the idea of rebirth. It is, and always has been, a traditional Buddhist teaching.

If we examine our own experience deeply, we see that the process of re-becoming takes place in the context of a single lifetime. In effect, we seem to die and be reborn all the time. Always becoming anew – we are never entirely the same from one day to the next. Looked at in this way, the view that the volitions which determine the way in which we re-become continue to operate after our death seems no more preposterous than the idea which our western conditioning leads us to take for granted – that somehow, out of nothing, consciousness comes into being for the first time somewhere between birth and conception. Although we may accept this, and even perhaps think of it as the 'scientific' view, it really is no more than a doctrine of miraculous apparition: from nothing, consciousness emerges – a miracle! Perhaps the doctrine of rebirth is not so strange after all.

Along with the idea of rebirth is a thought which is very reassuring. No spiritual effort is ever wasted. All our efforts to grow are, in a manner of speaking, conserved, and will bear fruit in time. This means that everything we do counts, and it is always worth making an effort to be skilful.

In any event, it is not absolutely necessary to believe in rebirth in order to be a Buddhist. But if you don't, then you must believe that it is possible to gain Enlightenment in

THE FIVE PRECEPTS

The way in which we behave has *karmic* consequences which effect our progress along the Path. But to the extent that we are un-Enlightened we can't always be certain that our volitions are skilful – sometimes our true motives are unknown even to ourselves. Because of this we need ethical guidelines to follow, and the list of Five Precepts is one such guide. It describes the way in which an Enlightened person naturally and sponta- neously behaves and, it is said, if we want to gain Enlightenment, we should seek to emulate such behaviour, for by changing our behaviour, we change our level of conscious- ness.

The Precepts aren't rules or commandments. There is nobody watching over us to make sure we stay up to scratch. Unlike lists such as the Ten Commandments, they are not 'what all Buddhists have to do'. One adopts them entirely voluntarily, as 'training principles'. Different Buddhists adopt different sets of precepts, but the Five Precepts, here presented in translation from their classical Pali form, are the most common:

I undertake the training principle to abstain from killing.

I undertake the training principle to not take what has not
been given.

I undertake the training principle to abstain from sexual
misconduct.

I undertake the training principle to refrain from falsehood.

I undertake the training principle to abstain from intoxicants.

Some western Buddhists have formulated positive counter- parts to these:

With deeds of loving kindness, I purify my mind.

With open-handed generosity, I purify my mind.

With stillness, simplicity and contentment, I purify my body.

With truthful communication I purify my speech.

With mindfulness, clear and radiant, I purify my mind.

As guidelines for training, the precepts are the extension of the process of Going for Refuge to the Three Jewels into the realm of daily life. They effectuate one's Going for Refuge by giving it practical expression. It is not just that one would *like* to move towards Enlightenment – by adopting the precepts we begin to change our behaviour so that it accords with our ideals. Just as there are four levels of Going for Refuge, so there are four corresponding levels at which one can practise the precepts:

At the Ethnic level the precepts are simply the rules of conduct of a group or society. As such they simply form part of conventional morality and are not adopted as rules for training on the spiritual path. At the Provisional level, newcomers to Buddhism adopt the precepts and try to live by them in order to gain a better understanding of what Buddhism is all about – trying them out in practice to see how they affect their lives. At the Effective level one is committed to living by the precepts and, although still caught up in *samsara*, still subject to acts of unskilfulness, one makes a consistent effort to live ethically. At the Real level one's actions naturally accord with the precepts. They are an expression of the way one *is*. Thus, the precepts describe the natural, free and spontaneous behaviour of members of the *Arya* Sangha.

1. *I undertake the training principle to abstain from killing. With deeds of loving kindness, I purify my mind.*

To be deprived of life is to be simultaneously deprived of everything which one holds dear. The will-to-live is common to all living things and to go against it is the most fundamental contradiction of the Golden Rule – *do to others as you would have them do to you.*

> All living beings are terrified of punishment; all
> fear death. Making comparison of others with oneself, one
> should neither kill nor cause to kill.

> All living beings are terrified of punishment; to
> all, life is dear. Making comparison of others with oneself,
> one should neither kill nor cause to kill.[2]

Buddhism extends the Golden Rule beyond the exclusive domain of mankind. It respects the will-to-life of all sentient beings.

When we kill, or harm another in any conscious way, we stop identifying with them as living beings – we see them only as objects, intrinsically separate from ourselves. This hardens the subject/object dichotomy and forces us back on to ourselves in a state of painful constriction. Thus, when we kill, we not only deprive another of that which is most precious to them, but we also harm ourselves. Love, the emotional identification of others with ourselves, diffuses the boundaries between us and the world, leaving us with a richer, broader experience of life itself.

Buddhists not only refrain from murder and other acts of violence, they also don't have abortions or counsel others to have them. They usually practice vegetarianism, are concerned for the environment and the well-being of other species and do not support trade in arms or any other product which harms living beings.

2. *I undertake the training principle to not take what has not been given. With open-handed generosity, I purify my mind.*

Just as we don't want to die, so we don't want to be forcibly parted from our possessions. What we own is a major part of our ego-identity and forcibly depriving someone of their property is a form of violence against them. Not only should we not take another person's property, but we should also not take their time or energy, unless it is freely offered.

Instead of taking, we can learn to give. Our fundamental orientation is to preserve our ego-identity by incorporating into it what we think will conduce to its security and well-being. This fundamental drive, which keeps us bound up in *samsara* and is the source of all our suffering, can gradually be changed through the conscious practice of generosity. Giving is the natural counter-part of non-violence and, just as the Buddhist Path can be seen as a training in non-violence, it is also a training in generosity. By cultivating generosity we begin to undo the bonds of egocentricity.

3. I undertake the training principle to abstain from sexual misconduct. With stillness, simplicity and contentment, I purify my body.

The Buddhist scriptures have very little to say on the subject of sex. Monks and nuns take a precept of chastity, and their monastic codes go into great detail about what kinds of act this precludes, but for those who are not living monastic lives not much is said. Usually this precept is interpreted as implying an abstention from rape, adultery and abduction, but there is clearly more to it than that.

Sex is a very important issue for all of us. The sexual instinct is very strong, and drives us to all kinds of strange behaviour. One thing that marks Buddhist culture, however, is that it has never sought to control sexuality by means of guilt, and on visiting some of the countries of Asia one finds them refreshingly guilt-free.

Buddhism doesn't discriminate between people on the basis of their sexual preferences. You can be heterosexual, homosexual, onanistic, transvestite or celibate. Nor has Buddhism ever ennobled the nuclear family. Marriage is not a sacrament in Buddhism; it is simply a social contract, and if one looks at the various Buddhist cultures around the world one finds socially accepted instances of monogamy, polygamy and polyandry. These are just different ways of arranging your life.

The important thing is that one doesn't harm other people by one's sexual behaviour or put a disproportionate emphasis on the value of sex itself. We live in a culture which places a massively disproportionate emphasis on sex – it is at the centre of so many people's lives. In Going for Refuge to the Three Jewels, however, one begins to move sex from the centre to the periphery of one's life and to decrease one's attachment to it.

The tension of sexual polarization and sexual desire hardens the subject/object duality. In a state of sexual arousal we see the person who is the object of our sexual desire as just that – an object. For many of us, our consciousness is never so hardened into a state of anxious separateness as when we are sexually aroused, especially if our sexual desire is frustrated. The opposite of this state is contentment – a state of being at ease with oneself and with the world which comes about not through the satisfaction of desire but ultimately through its non-arising.

4. *I undertake the training principle to refrain from falsehood.*
With truthful communication I purify my speech.

Human culture is made up in large part from the interwoven fabric of human communication, and for communication to be meaningful it must also be true. If we cannot have faith that what is being communicated is, in an ordinary sense, true, then society rapidly breaks down.

To lie is therefore to commit an act of violence against society. But when we lie, we also diminish ourselves. In most cases we lie in order to protect our ego-identity. By lying, we are thrust back into self-protectiveness, perpetuating a process whereby we circle within the narrow sphere of self-preoccupation.

Lying is also an act of violence against other individuals. By keeping the truth from them they are thrust into a fog of unreality. In Going for Refuge to the Buddha, we Go for Refuge to One who discovered and embodies the truth of things. The Dharma is that truth, and the Sangha are all those men and women who have made that truth their own. Untruth is the very opposite to the intentions of Buddhism as a whole.

5. *I undertake the training principle to abstain from intoxicants.*
With mindfulness, clear and radiant, I purify my mind.

Mental clarity is one of the qualities most prized in Buddhism. It is the means by which we finally penetrate the fog of delusion which is the source of universal suffering. Through clarity of mind we begin to free ourselves from the bonds of ignorance and become able to help others do the same.

Buddhist meditation practice is centred on the development of mental and emotional clarity. It gives rise to feelings of joy and liberation as the oppressive fog of confusion begins to lift. As one becomes increasingly committed to developing and sustaining clear states of mind, one naturally becomes less inclined to sacrifice one's hard-won clarity for the sake of a few glasses of alcohol. At the same time, as one's sensitivity increases as a result of meditation practice, one becomes increasingly conscious of the toxic side-effects of alcohol on the system.

A modern list of intoxicants would include not only drink and drugs, but all those activities which dull, confuse, or derange the mind. It can be intoxicating to be in the crowd at a football match or a discotheque. Too much television numbs the mind. Even shopping can be an intoxicating habit.

The habitual use of intoxicants leads to dependence. If one takes a glass of whisky to relax every evening, then eventually one can't relax without it. Through practising Buddhism, one learns in time to relax and simply enjoy one's current mental state without recourse to intoxicants.

Once one has experienced the bliss of meditative absorption, the pleasures of intoxication are like cheap daubs hung up for sale on the railings outside a great art gallery. Why be distracted by these when so many treasures lie waiting within?

References

1) See Willson, Martin. *Re-birth and the Western Buddhist*, Wisdom Publications, 1984, and Sangharakshita, *Who is the Buddha?* Windhorse Publications, 1994.

2) From the *Dhammapada*, verses 129–130, transl. Sangharakshita (unpublished).

MEDITATION

We have no fixed self. We're just a constantly changing flux of conditions, loosely bundled together into an identifiable pattern we call 'me'.

This process of change can be random – we can just be blown along, reacting to circumstances as they occur: blindly responding with craving to pleasant feelings, with aversion to unpleasant ones, all the time caught up in the delusion that somehow it will be possible to get what we really want from the changing stream of circumstances and then everything will be just right, forever.

Or we can live more consciously. Having caught at least a glimpse of the delusive nature of the idea that craving and aversion can produce a final, unchanging set of circumstances, where everything will be just right forever, we can set out to free ourselves from bondage to that delusion. By working to transform craving into generosity, aversion into compassion and delusion into wisdom, we can begin to expand our awareness so that it no longer circles about itself, confined within the hard, cold, isolating boundaries of egocentricity.

In the previous chapter I showed how our mental states effect, and are effected by, our behaviour. In this chapter I look at how we can change the quality of our mental states by working on them directly in meditation, and I will show how this can help us to cultivate wisdom – a direct, intuitive apprehension of the nature of reality itself.

The traditional term for meditation is *bhavana* – mental and emotional development. It is the systematic attempt to bring about certain desired changes in one's mental state by working directly upon the mind in all its dimensions. There are a large number of different Buddhist meditation practices, but broadly speaking they can be divided into two main categories: *samatha* and *vipassana*.

Samatha meditations are intended to develop higher mental states – marked by integration, concentration, calm, and positive emotion – as well as states of deep meditative absorption; whilst *vipassana* meditations are intended to develop insight into things as they really are.

We will look at each of these in turn. But first a warning. You can no more learn to meditate by reading a description of it in a book than you can learn to drive by reading the handbook of a car. I hope to give some idea here of what Buddhist meditation practice is about, but I am not setting out to teach meditation – for that there is no substitute for personal instruction from a qualified teacher.

SAMATHA

I remember the first time I sat down to meditate. It was chaos.

I'd have a thought about what I did the day before ... then a quick thought about dinner ... then a dash of anger about what someone said to me ... then remember a scene from a film I saw the week before ... then notice a sense of physical discomfort in my shoulder ... then have a little wave of panic about an appointment I had to remember for the next day ... then plan what I was going to have for breakfast ... then feel a little burst of warmth for the funny fellow who runs that vegetable stall on the market ... then wonder whether coffee really was bad for me ... then catch a random glimpse of a half-remembered scene from Paris ... then wonder whether language really did delineate experience ... then hope tomorrow would be sunny ... then wonder about my friend (what she said) ... then feel irritable with my knee .... All this in less than five minutes.

It is quite common to have this sort of experience when first learning to meditate (that is, if you don't just fall asleep), and the really sobering realization is that this is how our minds are working all the time, not only when we stop to look at what is happening in them. They work like this when we're not looking as well.

Because, as we saw earlier, we don't have a single, integrated self. Rather, we live our lives in varying degrees of 'dis-integration'. We comprise a number of fragmentary 'selves', all vying for attention, competing for temporary control of the psycho-physical organism we call ourselves. And, if we want to begin to take some control over the overall direction of our lives, so that we can begin to replace unskilful volitions with skilful volitions, then we first of all need to develop some rudimentary integration.

Just as different physical exercises develop the body in different ways, so different meditation techniques develop different aspects of psyche. The Mindfulness of Breathing practice develops calm and integration.

THE MINDFULNESS OF BREATHING

Like all the meditation practices I will be describing, you begin the Mindfulness of Breathing practice by going to a quiet spot where you won't be disturbed, and sitting down in an upright meditation posture. Most people sit on the floor, either with their buttocks on a stack of cushions about 9 inches high, and their legs crossed with their knees touching the floor, or, if your knees don't naturally touch the floor when sitting like this, you can kneel, with your knees on the floor and your buttocks supported by a low bench (about 6 or 9 inches high) or a small stack of cushions. You can, if necessary, also sit upright on a firm chair, such as a dining chair.

With a firm base such as this, your body naturally becomes upright and your neck and shoulders relax. Your hands lie lightly cupped, one in the other, in your lap. Your eyes can be closed or half-open and your head is upright – comfortably balanced on top of the spine. This posture is poised, alert, relaxed and energetic.

The Mindfulness of Breathing practice is divided into four stages of more or less equal length. Most people begin by practising for 10 or 20 minutes in all. Those who keep up regular practise usually go on to sit for 40 minutes or more.

You begin by attending to the process of breathing itself. Not trying to interfere with the process, not making the breaths longer or shorter, you just attend to the process of breathing, becoming increasingly aware of it. In the first stage, to help keep your attention on the breath, just count each breath, at the end of every out-breath. Breathe in, breathe out, and count 'one'. Breathe in, breathe out, and count 'two' ... and so on up to '10', and then go back to 'one', and so the cycle continues. Counting the out breaths from one to 10, over and over.

In the second stage the practice becomes slightly more subtle. Rather than counting after the out-breath, you count before the in-breath, from one to 10, over and over.

In the third stage, stop counting and just watch the breath, attending to the process of breathing. Just letting it flow and sitting with it, being fully attentive to it.

In the fourth stage, you focus your attention at that point

where you first become aware of breath entering your body. It might be a slight tickle at the tip of the nose, or inside the nose or at the back of the throat. Wherever this sensation occurs, locate it and just attend fully to it, as it changes with every passing moment.

If you can allow your attention to rest, happily and undistractedly, on such a subtle moment of experience for even only five minutes, then you will have become highly concentrated. Your energies will all be flowing together and you will be in a very relaxed and highly refined mental state.

Although this may sound simple, it can be a little difficult to do at first. It's quite common, for instance, to find oneself counting 32, 33, 34 ... having quite forgotten to return to one after reaching 10. And most people find that, even if they can put aside the sheer physical discomfort of all their accumulated bodily tension, their minds just wander off on courses of their own, oblivious to any attempt to keep them focused on the breath. But perseverance helps.

There are a number of techniques one can employ to work in meditation.[1] For example, we saw in Chapter 2 in the section on Perfect Effort that there are five hindrances which obstruct one's efforts to develop skilful mental states. But there are also four traditional methods for eradicating these hindrances. An experienced meditation instructor will be able to help one negotiate the hidden reefs which can wreck our attempts to gain concentration.

The rewards for persistent effort in meditation are substantial. One grows calmer, clearer, more relaxed and more directed in one's intentions. One may also experience the pleasures of the *dhyanas* – superconscious states of meditative absorption.

As explained earlier, we don't have a single, unitary self: we're just a loose bundle of selves, tied together by a vague sense of self-identity, and these selves are often in states of conflict with one another. To progress along the spiritual path we need to bring these different selves together, into a more harmonious, integrated whole. We can integrate ourselves 'horizontally' at the psychological level of being, getting our different 'selves' to become aware of one another, getting them to co-operate more harmoniously, and we can integrate ourselves 'vertically' by experiencing the heights and depths of our more 'spiritual' potential.

There are four *dhyanas*, each successively more refined. The first two pertain to the dimension of horizontal, or psychological integration. The last two, in which one's experience is less definitely dualized (divided into experiencing subject and experienced object) pertain to vertical integration.

The *dhyanas* don't arise in dependence upon anything external to us. They are states of extreme blissful happiness which are the psycho-physical reflex of deep absorption.

The first *dhyana* is a state of integration characterized by an absence of the hindrances, all one's previously conflicting psycho-physical energies having come into a state of at least temporary unification. One is simply happy – being who one is, doing what one is doing. There is still a certain amount of mental activity present, but it doesn't distract from the meditation and one just sits, very happy and contented, maybe feeling an occasional shudder of rapture.

If one can stay with that state, without falling into distraction, then thinking begins to die away, rapture calms down, one becomes even more aware and alert, and moves into the second *dhyana*.

This is the state of inspiration. Here the mind becomes like a vast clear lake of sparklingly pure water: calm and tranquil, and, as if from nowhere, a spring of fresh water, a spring of inspiration, constantly bubbles up into the lake, feeding and expanding it. It is a state of intense delight. If one stays relaxed, clear, undistracted and receptive to the very subtle movements and changes that are now taking place in one's mind, the water from the lake can, as it were, overflow its boundaries and one moves into the third *dhyana*.

Here the boundaries of the psycho-physical organism have become highly attenuated. One hardly experiences oneself as having a body at all. Fully absorbed in meditation, one begins to have a first taste of the blissful possibilities of radiant limitlessness.

Entering the fourth *dhyana*, even bliss dies away. Subjectivity itself has become almost completely attenuated. There is just the intense radiance of a state of equanimity, even more pleasurable than pleasure. It is a state of perfect harmony and equilibrium.

Such are the heights of *samatha*. With a mind clarified, refreshed and made pliable by experiences like these, one can begin to contemplate the nature of reality and see it in its depths, unmediated by distracting subjectivity. Such heights are not easy to scale, but others have gone before us – the *dhyanas* can be attained, and, given a little time and supportive conditions, most people can quite easily gain some experience of the first two at least.

One of the factors which keeps us from experiencing the *dhyanas* spontaneously, whenever we sit down and close our eyes, is the tendency we all have towards habitual negative emotions – craving, anger, irritability, jealousy and so on. The *metta bhavana* is a meditation practice which is designed to transform these. In particular, it aims at the development of *metta* – loving kindness.

Bhavana, as explained, means 'development' and is a synonym for meditation, but there isn't a satisfactory translation for the word *metta* in English. It means something like 'loving-kindness', but that can easily be associated with sentimentality. One could use the word 'love', but that has come to have connotations of exclusivity and neurotic attachment. *Metta*, on the other hand, is a feeling of universal, all-pervading, well-wishing. It is a broad, inclusive state of warm, intense goodwill.

The practice is divided into five stages of more or less equal length. In the first stage you try to cultivate feelings of *metta* towards yourself. There are various techniques you can use to do this, and personal meditation instruction is the best way to learn these.

You sit in the first stage simply trying to feel feelings of warmth, goodwill, kindness and well-wishing towards yourself. You don't merely think about feelings of *metta* in this practice, you try to feel them, in the heart, not in the head.

In the second stage you call to mind a friend. Someone who is not a sexual partner, and of a similar age to oneself (for otherwise your feelings of *metta* may be confused with parental, filial or sexual feelings). Bearing this friend in mind, you try to develop ever stronger feelings of *metta* towards them.

In the third stage, call to mind a 'neutral' person. Someone with whom you have fairly regular contact, but for whom you don't feel any strong feelings one way or the other. Trying to get a sense of their humanity, you try to feel feelings of *metta* towards them.

In the fourth stage, you call to mind an enemy, or someone with whom your communication is a little abrasive, or with whom communication has broken down, and you try to develop feelings of *metta* towards them.

In the fifth and final stage you bring to mind all four people: yourself, your friend, the neutral person and the enemy, and you try to feel feelings of warmth and *metta* for all four, equally and impartially. From there, you begin to radiate that feeling of *metta* outwards. Beginning with everyone in your immediate locale, then reaching out into the neighbourhood, the town, the county, the country, the continent, the world – radiating feelings of warmth and *metta* to all living beings everywhere.

The *metta bhavana* is a powerfully transforming practice. Once one has a little experience of it, most people find that they can use it almost without fail to bring about an improvement in their current mental state. Regularly practised over a sufficient period of time, you come to develop deep reserves of *metta* which you can call upon more or less at will.

VIPASSANA

However refined, however strong the states of *samatha* you cultivate might be, they are nonetheless still subject to mundane conditions. When the conditions which gave rise to them pass, they evaporate like the morning dew. The only way to escape from the gravitational pull of mundane conditions is by the development of *vipassana* – direct, experiential insight into the nature of things as they really are.

There are a number of practices designed to generate such an insight, but they all require a substantial grounding in *samatha* in order to be effective. Unless you are sufficiently integrated you cannot bring your whole being to the *vipassana* practice. Without that, *vipassana* practices might be useful to some extent, but they won't be irreversibly transformative. And unless you have developed a high level of positive emotion, the existential shock which *vipassana* practice can produce might throw you seriously off course. For the intention of *vipassana* is

to bring about the direct experience of *shunyata* – emptiness.
Vipassana practices are designed to enable us to penetrate the myth of substantiality and to experience directly for ourselves the unsatisfactory, impermanent and insubstantial nature of all phenomena – thus freeing us, once and for all, from bondage to *samsara*.

One such practice is the Contemplation of the Six Elements

THE SIX ELEMENT PRACTICE

According to Indian tradition, the material world is made up of four great elements: earth, water, fire and air. All material objects, including our own bodies, can be reduced to these elements. When we add to these the elements of space and consciousness, they give us, in ascending order of refinement, a complete description of the make-up of the whole psychophysical organism. Apart from these elements there is no 'self'. We construct our fixed sense of ourselves from the Six Elements. If we want to free ourselves from that delusion and experientially apprehend the true nature of things, then we must let go of our attachment to the Six Elements altogether. That is what one sets out to do in the Six Element Practice.

You start by establishing a foundation of mindfulness and emotional positivity, and then you begin with the Earth element. You reflect that everything in yourself that is hard and solid, everything that offers resistance: your bones, hair, skin and teeth; all of these things are just part of the great earth element in the universe. You can't hold on to them forever. When you die, they will just return to the earth. You have only borrowed them temporarily. They are not 'you'. You shouldn't identify yourself with them. Since they are not 'yours' you might as well allow them to return to the great earth element in the universe. And so you let go of all the manifestations of the earth element in your body. You cease to cling to them, cease to identify yourself with them. You just let them go, and feel a consequent lightening and sense of liberation.

Going on to the Water element, you consider that, in part, you are made of water. All the fluids in your body are just various transformations of the water element. But these fluids don't really belong to you. You can't hold on to them forever. You have just borrowed them from the great water element in the universe and when you die they will return to that great water element. Blood, tears, perspiration, urine – none of your bodily fluids has any permanence, none of them is finally your own. So, again, you give them up. Allow them to simply be part of the great water element in the universe. They are not 'you'.

You move on to the Fire element and feelings of physical warmth. When you die, your corpse almost immediately becomes cold. This warmth you now feel is not 'yours', it is temporary. You have it only on loan, for a short while. So you let go of it, stop feeling attached to it, stop allowing it to establish one of the boundaries of your being.

Next, you reflect on the Air element. You breathe in and breathe out, but you can never hold on to the air in your body. It is in constant motion. It is simply the great air element in the universe which you use for a very short while. So give it up. Let go. And by now your sense of yourself has become highly refined and attenuated. You don't identify yourself with your body in the way that you usually do. Although you continue to experience the body, you're no longer so attached to that experience and there is a more refined quality to your experience.

Next you reflect on the element of Space. The space which you currently occupy is always changing. When all the material elements have been let go of, what space do you occupy? This shape you have is not 'you'. It is merely an appearance, created by the temporary coming together of the material elements. When you let go of them, you also let go of your shape. It becomes just part of the space of the universe.

By now you experience very little sense of limit.

You reflect that your consciousness is not fixed and finite. If you don't 'own' your body, how can it be the final location of your consciousness? Where *are* the boundaries of your consciousness. What makes it 'yours'? You have no fixed and final self at all. So just let go of the discursive process of self-identification, and you experience ...

Well, you experience what you experience. At this stage we have completely gone beyond the possibilities of linguistic expression. Of its very nature, one cannot describe such an experience. It is beyond all limiting conceptions.

VISUALIZATION PRACTICE

Another approach to *vipassana* is the practice of visualization. There are a large number of these, one of the most popular being the visualization of one or another of the archetypal Buddha or Bodhisattva forms.

Here you begin as before, establishing mindfulness and positivity, and then you visualize in front of you a clear blue sky, extending in all directions of space. Then, within the sky, you conjure up the image of one or another of the transcendental Buddha or Bodhisattva forms which are made entirely of light, glowing like a rainbow. One contemplates the image for a time, perhaps recites devotional verses, recites the *mantra* associated with the image, receives blessings from the Buddha or Bodhisattva, and then one resolves the image back into the blue sky. At this point one can reflect that just as the visualized image appears from emptiness and returns to emptiness, so too do we and all phenomena.

There are an enormous number of variations on this type of

meditation, but tradition asserts that they cannot be effectively practised without one first having been initiated into such practice in the context of a teacher/disciple relationship. Only then will the essence of the practice be communicated.

Like all *vipassana* practices, visualization is not for the spiritual dilettante. It is a means of beginning to contact other dimensions of reality – a process which should not be trifled with. Ideally, you should avoid these levels of practice until such time as your Going for Refuge has become truly effective, and you can practice them within the context of a supportive spiritual community.

FORMLESS MEDITATIONS

So far we have looked mainly at meditation practices which have a particular object and a certain amount of structure. There are also, however, practices which have very little structure and no particular object.

There are a large number of different formless meditations taught in the different Buddhist traditions – *dzogchen*, *mahamudra*, *zazen*, to name but a few. Perhaps we are most familiar with the term *zazen*, which comes from the Zen tradition (the other two are Tibetan). There is very little one can say about these. With *dzogchen*, it is said, one simply enters into an unmediated experience of the innate purity of mind. *Mahamudra* is the 'effortless experience of emptiness' and *zazen* is 'just sitting'.

But don't get the impression that because these are formless they are therefore easy. Progress in formless meditation takes years of regular, dedicated effort. For formless meditation is not just sitting and drifting.

Here, Yasutani Roshi communicates something of the relaxed but focused intensity of the mind of one properly engaged in 'just sitting':

[It] is the mind of somebody facing death. Let us imagine that you are engaged in a duel of swordsmanship of the kind that used to take place in ancient Japan. As you face your opponent you are unceasingly watchful, set, ready. Were you to relax your vigilance even momentarily, you would be cut down instantly. A crowd gathers to see the fight. Since you are not blind you see them from the corner of your eye, and since you are not deaf you hear them. But not for an instant is your mind captured by these impressions.[2]

DEVOTION AND RITUAL

Another highly effective way of working to bring about desired changes in your state of mind is through the practice of ritual and devotion. All schools of Buddhism engage in these – bowing before shrines and images of the Buddha; making offerings of flowers, lights and incense; and chanting devotional verses. From the exquisitely formalized rituals of Zen to the imaginative abundance of Tibetan tantra, Buddhists over the centuries have devised a wide variety of means for engaging their emotions and imaginations in the process of transformation.

There are several dimensions to this. To begin with, you can achieve very little, in any field of endeavour, unless you have devotion. Successful artists are devoted to their art, athletes to their sport, school teachers to their pupils. Without such emotional engagement their achievements will never be more than mediocre. In the same way, unless you are devoted to the Three Jewels, imaginatively engaged with them and serious about spiritual progress you will never really get anywhere. Buddhist rituals are designed to bring about that quality of engagement.

As you begin to practice, and as the Dharma begins to affect your life for the better, you begin to feel deep gratitude to the Buddha, for having made the Dharma available. You feel reverence for the Dharma, which is having such profound effects in your life. And you feel gratitude to the *Arya* Sangha, for keeping the Dharma alive. Devotional practice is a way of expressing this gratitude.

Devotional practice is also a means of self-transcendence. Imaginatively engaging with the awesome heights and depths of Enlightenment, you leave your petty, limiting concerns behind for a time and participate, at least to some extent, in a drama of cosmic dimensions.

Buddhist ritual is rich in symbolic significance. Participating in it you begin to become attuned to symbolism itself. The effect of this is to enrich your sensibility, heighten your aesthetic awareness and open up to the poetry inherent in every moment of existence.

References

1) For a much fuller treatment of these, see Kamalashila, *Meditation, the Buddhist Way of Tranquillity and Insight*, Windhorse Publications, 1992.

2) ed. Kapleau, Philip. *The Three Pillars of Zen: Teaching, Practice and Enlightenment*, New York, 1980.

THE SPREAD AND DEVELOPMENT OF BUDDHISM

The Emperor Ashoka, who lived from 269 to 232 BCE, ruled the Mauryan kingdom of northern India and did much to consolidate the position of Buddhism. A gifted ruler, he began his imperial career with extensive territorial ambitions, but a costly victory, where many on both sides lost their lives, brought him to an acute psychological crisis which resulted in his embracing Buddhism. He began a 'reign of the Dharma', undertaking journeys through his realm to establish virtue. He propagated pacifism and vegetarianism, and forbade animal sacrifice.

Ashoka sent Buddhist missions to the Greek kingdoms to his west, but there is no record of their having been received. He had more success in Sri Lanka – sending his son Mahinda there as a Buddhist missionary in the first known instance of the Dharma spreading across the sea.

Three more centuries were to elapse before Buddhism finally penetrated the whole Indian sub-continent. It then began to expand into Greater Asia. From Gandara, an Indo-Greek kingdom to the north west of India, Buddhism gradually filtered into central Asia, and from there it followed the Silk Road into China, where the first established Buddhist community we know of emerged around 150 CE. Gradually Buddhism spread throughout China, increasing in strength and influence until, under the T'ang Dynasty (618–907 CE), it entered a Golden Age – truly Chinese forms of Buddhism: Avatamsaka, Tien Tai, Pure Land and Ch'an all began to emerge in this period. As Chinese civilization spread, so too did Buddhism, entering Vietnam, Korea and Japan around the sixth century.

Around about the seventh century, Buddhism was introduced into Tibet from the Swat valley to its west and from India to its south, but it was another 200 years before it began to establish itself, giving rise in time to perhaps the most spiritually creative culture the world has ever seen.

In Sri Lanka, Mahinda's mission in the second century BCE had been successful and Buddhism has existed on the island, although often very precariously, from then until the present day. For many years Theravada, Mahayana and Tantric Buddhism all exerted an influence as royal patronage swayed this way and that. Finally, in the twelfth century, the other forms were suppressed and the Theravada became dominant.

Although the countries of south-east Asia had to some extent come under the influence of Mahayana Buddhism, which had spread from India or China, missions from Sri Lanka eventually helped to establish Theravada Buddhism in the region, and it is now the predominant form of Buddhism in Burma, Thailand, Cambodia and Laos.

In the thirteenth century Buddhism began to die out in India, partly as a result of the Muslim invasion. With a fanatical hatred of what appeared to them to be 'idolatry', the Muslim conquerors burned down monasteries, libraries and universities, killing large numbers of monks. The pacific Buddhist monks offered little resistance and, with the destruction of the Buddhist centres of monastic training, Brahmanism, which had to a large extent already absorbed Mahayana Buddhist concepts and imagery, now began to absorb popular Buddhism

itself. Seven centuries were to elapse before Buddhism began to
revive in India.

BUDDHISM TODAY

The modern age has dawned very rapidly for most Buddhist cultures. Before the 1950s Tibet was to all intents and purposes a medieval feudal society, with most of its inhabitants living in ignorance of such phenomena as motor cars and radios; most other Asian countries were still largely agrarian, and Buddhists of different nationalities were only very dimly aware of one another's existence. The globalization which we take for granted throughout the world today has only emerged in the last few decades, and the situation which now prevails all around the world is almost unrecognizably different from that which we would have found as little as 50 years ago.

In Japan, periods of instability which have followed the industrial revolution have seen the development of hundreds of so-called New Religions. Sometimes comprising no more than a few hundred people, several of these derived their beliefs from one or another reading of the traditional Buddhist scriptures. A few of the New Religions have grown to be very large indeed: Rissho Kosei-kai and Sokka Gakai International (SGI), for example, number their followers in millions.

Both of the latter organizations are off-shoots of Nichiren Buddhism, which traces its ancestry back to the militant thirteenth century figure of the same name. For Nichiren, as for his present day followers, the quintessence of the Dharma is contained in the *gohonzon* – a *mantra*-like invocation: '*Nam-myoho-reng-kyo*' ('Homage to the mystic Law of *The Lotus Sutra*'), the chanting of which, Sokka Gakai say, brings all boons, both spiritual and material.

Perhaps because of the ease and simplicity of this teaching,

Nichiren Buddhism, in the form of Sokka Gakai International, has attracted an enormous following both within Japan and without, where it is best known for its celebrity followers: the singers Tina Turner and Boy George, the Italian footballer Roberto Baggio, as well as many minor celebrities from the world of fashion and the media. It is not clear to what extent these are aware of Nichiren's own extraordinary militancy: *All the [Pure Land] and Zen temples ... should be burned to the ground and their priests taken to Yui beach to have their heads cut-off!*[1], he once advised a Japanese court. Nor is it clear to what extent other Buddhists can accept as a true profession of the Dharma a teaching which claims to spring from 'the only Buddha of this age', Nichiren himself, and which believes that in proselytization the ends always justify the means.

Whilst the New Religions have grown and expanded, the current century has not treated the more traditional forms of Japanese Buddhism very kindly. The war left the monasteries financially ruined through General MacArthur's 'land reform' and, following the economic reconstruction of the country, materialism flourishes as never before. Loyalty to a single religion, moreover, has never played a major part in the Japanese cultural make-up and Buddhism, which thus co-exists in modern national life with Shinto and Christianity, is confined in great part to the conduct of rites of passage – especially funerals.

With Buddhism in decline in Japan a small handful of *roshis* began to consider the necessity of spreading the Japanese Zen approach beyond the borders which had confined it for eight centuries. Nyogen Senzaki, Sokei-an Sasaki, Nakagawa Soen, Haku'un Yasutani, Sunyru Suzuki, Taisan Shimano Eido and Taizan Maezumi between them played an enormous part in establishing Zen Buddhism in America and, to a lesser extent, in Europe.

Japanese Pure Land Buddhism has also made its way to the United States, where the Buddhist Churches of America mainly serve the needs of the Japanese ethnic population.

In Korea Zen Buddhism thrives under the name of *Son*, but it is subject to the encroachment of aggressive Christian missionary activity and, as in Hong Kong, Taiwan, Thailand, Singapore and Malaysia, a burgeoning consumerism fed by the south-east Asian 'economic miracle'. Korean Zen, however, has come to the west, particularly in the shape of the Kwan Um Zen School, which was founded by Seung Sahn Sunim in 1983 and which is adapted to the needs of westerners.

In Vietnam, Cambodia and Laos, war shattered what were once thriving Buddhist cultures. Nothing illustrates this more vividly than the pictures of calm Buddhist monks and nuns, driven to the desperate act of self-immolation to draw the world's attention to the oppression which Buddhism suffered at the hands of the South Vietnamese Roman Catholic dictator Ngo Dinh Diem in 1963.

Three years later, the Vietnamese Zen master, Thich Nhat Hanh journeyed to Europe and America to try to communicate the effect that the war in Vietnam was having on ordinary people, and to promote the cause of peace. Since those days Nhat Hanh has largely remained in the west, where he has been a tireless activist for peace – teaching an approach to Buddhism which emphasizes social responsibility and pacifism based on the practice of mindful awareness.

In China, the Cultural Revolution dealt a near-fatal blow to a Buddhism which had already been weakened by centuries of political turmoil. As in Japan, the Chinese have rarely been loyal to one religion alone and today what remnants of Buddhism there are amongst the Chinese populations of Asia are often found intermingled with elements of Confucianism, Taoism, and local animism.

Even so, a variety of more 'orthodox' Chinese Buddhist institutions continue to thrive, particularly in Taiwan and the United States. Ch'an Buddhism has also found its way to the west, but as yet it is not as popular as Zen.

In Inner Mongolia, a part of China, Buddhism experienced the same fate as in China itself, whilst in Outer Mongolia, for many years part of the former USSR, it suffered tremendous depredations at the hands of Josef Stalin and his successors.

Of all the Buddhist countries which have suffered at the hands of oppressive regimes in this century, none has caught the popular imagination as much as Tibet, which the west conceives as a land so close to the sky that the natural inclination of her people is to pray, a high place of crystalline purity, sacred mystery, worldly innocence and spiritual mastery: a Utopian Shangri-la beyond the lost horizon.[2]

Although this portrayal ignores the dark underside of Tibetan feudal life, where the struggle for temporal power was necessarily inseparable from many aspects of institutionalized religious life, nonetheless Tibet was a thriving Buddhocracy before the brutal Chinese invasion of 1959. Perhaps more than any other culture in history, life in the country was informed by truly spiritual values, and in consequence it produced a large number of very highly attained spiritual adepts.

The Chinese, however, have treated Tibetan culture and religion with a cruel, oppressive disdain – destroying the monasteries and killing or imprisoning monks and nuns. In 1959 the Dalai Lama fled into exile in India where many thousands of Tibetans have since joined him. With irrepressible optimism and cheerfulness, Tibetan Buddhism today lives on in thriving Tibetan refugee communities in India, especially around Dharamsala, where the Dalai Lama himself is based, and the great monastic institutions of Tibet have been reconstructed in exile, albeit in a much reduced form. Tibetan style Buddhism also continues to flourish to some extent in Nepal, as well as in Sikkim, Bhutan and Ladakh.

Although emphatically not the Buddhist equivalent of the Pope, as he is sometimes mistakenly thought to be, the Dalai Lama occupies a unique position in the Tibetan Buddhist world. Since the seventeenth century his previous incarnations have ruled Tibet, and the current Dalai Lama, the fourteenth in succession, is effectively a head of state in exile. At the same time he is a highly qualified *lama* of the Gelugpa tradition and is thus called upon to bridge two worlds – the sacred and the secular: a task which he appears to perform with deceptive ease.

The Dalai Lama is regarded by the Tibetan people with awed affection – an attitude they share with some of his followers in the west. For although he likes to call himself 'a simple Tibetan monk', he has proved to be much more than that. As a tireless campaigner on behalf of the Tibetan people and for peace in general, he has gained a reputation for wisdom and integrity which few other modern statesmen share.

One of the positive effects of this Tibetan diaspora has been the spread of the Tibetan approach to Buddhism beyond the Himalayan region which had confined it for over a thousand years. There are now Tibetan Buddhist centres of all the major schools in most countries of the west. At last the spiritual riches which had been cultivated in a state of pristine isolation are being shared.

Burmese Buddhism, which came to be associated with Burmese nationalism in opposition to British imperial rule, today finds itself forced into compromise with the SLORC: the State Law and Order Restoration Committee, which currently rules the country. The SLORC brooks no opposition and expects, if not support, then at least passivity from the local Theravadin *bhikkhu* sangha. At times some monks have registered their protest at being expected to turn a blind eye to acts of genocide amongst the hill tribes, and other forms of institutional oppression, but they have been harshly dealt with.

Before the advent of SLORC, however, a few Burmese meditation masters – principally Mahasi Sayadaw and U Ba Khin – were partly responsible for the beginnings of a revival of the practice of meditation in the Theravadin Buddhist world. Their predominantly western lay disciples now teach meditation widely throughout the world, particularly under the auspices of the Insight Meditation Society, which is based in the United States.

In Thailand and Sri Lanka too, there is a strong connection between Buddhism and the state, and whereas this is largely ceremonial in Thailand, Sri Lanka has lately been subject to outbreaks of Buddhist religio-nationalism as the minority Tamil Hindus have fought for greater rights and recognition. The involvement of some Buddhist monks in the violent struggles of the last decade runs quite counter to all the teachings of Buddhism.

In both Thailand and Sri Lanka, however, a minority of monks follow 'the Forest Tradition' – avoiding the towns and dedicating themselves to meditation. Prominent amongst these was Ajahn Chah, whose followers in Thailand and the west have done much to revive the Forest Tradition. The American-born Ajahn Sumedho, one of Ajahn Chah's foremost disciples, has helped to found monasteries of that tradition in several parts of the west, most successfully in Britain.

In Thailand, Cambodia, India and Sri Lanka, some Buddhists are playing a significant part in developing forms of peaceful social activism. The recently deceased Thai monk, Buddhadasa Bhikkhu, was especially renowned for his efforts to propagate forms of Buddhist practice which address social and political, as well as transcendental realities; and in India Bahujan Hitay, the social work wing of the Western Buddhist Order, does valuable work in the new Buddhist community.

Perhaps one of the brightest points of light on the Asian Buddhist scene in this century has been the Buddhist revival in India. This was sparked off by Dr B.K.S. Ambedkar, the first Law Minister in independent India. Born into an Untouchable caste, Dr Ambedkar experienced severe oppression at the hands of caste Hindus throughout his formative years. Despite this he was the first Untouchable ever to matriculate, and he went on to achieve degrees from London and Columbia Universities, eventually qualifying as a barrister in London.

Although the Constitution of India, which he himself drafted, made the practice of Untouchability illegal, Ambedkar finally saw that despite all his struggles and campaigns, Hinduism would never grant equal status to the Untouchables, and he decided to seek a new religion for himself and his people. He eventually settled on Buddhism for four reasons: it was Indian in origin; it didn't ennoble poverty; it was based in reason; and it promoted liberty, equality and fraternity.

In 1956 Ambedkar publicly embraced Buddhism together with 400,000 of his followers. In the next few weeks several hundred thousand more joined them, and a movement had begun. Today there are over 10 million new Buddhists in India. Once the lowest of the low, deprived even of the opportunity to practise a religion, the new Indian Buddhists now have a future in a religion which asserts that all can raise themselves up, irrespective of their background, and which provides practical guidance for so doing. As a result they show immense reverence and gratitude towards the Buddha and Dr Ambedkar, whose peaceful revolution truly set them free.

But perhaps history will record that the most dramatic event in this century, so far as Buddhism is concerned, is its beginning to take root in the west, where the technologies of travel and communication, the particularities of the western psyche and the fact that all the major Buddhist schools are represented there, make for a situation unique in Buddhist history.

BUDDHISM IN THE WEST

In *The Awakening of the West*, the story of the encounter between Buddhism and western culture, Stephen Batchelor suggests that the western relationship to Buddhism has been marked by five attitudes: blind indifference, self-righteous rejection, rational knowledge, romantic fantasy and existential engagement.[3] This classification can be used in many ways.

Most obviously, it details the chronological stages in the encounter between Buddhism and the west, but it can also describe psychological strata within the western mind: even practising western Buddhists 'may still entertain romantic notions about enlightenment; attend a course to study Buddhism with rational objectivity from non-Buddhist professors; reject particular ideas as alien features of Asian culture; and be indifferent to aspects of the teachings that, they believe, do not concern them.'[4]

It can also be used to describe current attitudes to Buddhism in the west, where perhaps the majority of people remain blindly indifferent to Buddhism. There are fundamentalists of all hues who self-righteously reject it as well as non-Buddhist academics who specialize in an exclusively rational knowledge of it. Romantic fantasies about Buddhism abound in New Age circles and even in some Buddhist groups, where the first phase of existential engagement is often strongly marked by naiveté. And finally, there are experienced western Buddhist practitioners and teachers, whose existential engagement with the Teachings have given rise to significant spiritual insights.

Historically speaking, the period of blind indifference on the part of the west to Buddhism lasted until the thirteenth century during which period, with the exception of a few ancient Greeks, Europe had neither knowledge of nor interest in Asian culture. In the middle of that century, however, the threat of a Mongol invasion from the east startled the European powers into an awareness which extended beyond the boundaries of the Mediterranean. Envoys were sent to the court of the Khans, and explorers journeyed as far east as Ulan Bator and Peking. Their letters, journals and reports document the beginnings of the first European knowledge of Buddhism.

From then until the beginning of the eighteenth century the European attitude to Buddhism was almost entirely one of self-righteous rejection – what scant knowledge of it there was leading to its dismissal as a form of heathen idolatry.

The period between the latter part of the eighteenth century and the beginning of the twentieth century saw the start of the European 'construction' of Buddhism, for the word 'Buddhism' is a European invention for which no Asian equivalent exists. It came into usage for the first time around the 1830s, as European imperialists strove to make sense of the apparently diverse beliefs and practices which were current in Asia at the time. Gradually the word 'Buddhism' came to be distinguished from other new words (such as 'Hinduism'), and by the 1860s it began to be connected exclusively with the beliefs and practices of those people who followed the teachings of the Buddha. What the Europeans began to call 'Buddhism' had, until then, always been known to its various practitioners simply as 'the Dharma'.

Over this same period the western attitude to Buddhism split in two: one half dealt with Buddhism as a field of rational, scientific knowledge, whilst the other half turned it into an object of romantic fantasy. This division is perhaps more accurately spoken of as a spectrum.

At one extreme were the early scholars and translators. Towards the centre were artists and philosophers, such as Arthur Schopenhauer, whose enthusiasm for a partially understood Buddhism in turn infected his followers Richard Wagner and Friedrich Nietzsche. The New England 'Transcendentalists' led by Ralph Waldo Emerson dabbled in orientalism, and Henry Thoreau translated Eugene Burnouf's translation of *The Lotus Sutra* into English. In England, Sir Edwin Arnold's great poem *The Light of Asia* sold in the hundreds of thousands.

At the other end of the spectrum were romantic fantasists such as the early Theosophists, most prominent amongst whom was Madame Blavatsky, the Russian author of *Isis Unveiled*, and her American partner Colonel Henry Steel Olcott whose enthusiasm for Buddhism led them, in Sri Lanka in 1880, to become the first westerners to take the Three Refuges and Five Precepts, and thus publicly embrace Theravada Buddhism.

Only at the beginning of the twentieth century did the first small handful of westerners begin to engage with Buddhism as a path of practice which would address their individual existential concerns, and it was only in the 1960s that the first effective Buddhist spiritual communities began to arise in the west.

Between the 1960s and 1970s most of the Dharma teaching in the west was carried out by Asians – particularly by Japanese Roshis and Tibetan Rimpoches – although a small handful of westerners, who had travelled to the east to study Buddhism, had by then returned and were beginning to establish Buddhist groups of their own. Amongst these were Sangharakshita, the English founder of the Friends of the Western Buddhist Order (FWBO), Robert Aitken Roshi, who founded the Zen Diamond Sangha in Hawaii, and Philip Kapleau Roshi, founder of the Rochester Zen Center in New York State.

During the 1970s representatives from almost every extant Buddhist school in the world arrived in the west where they established urban Buddhist centres, rural retreat centres or peripatetic teaching programmes. From Tibet there were representatives of the Gelugpa, Kagyupa, Nyingmapa and Shakyapa schools. Japanese Soto and Rinzai Zen were well established and one could study Chinese Ch'an, Korean *Son* or Vietnamese *Thien* in many European and American cities, whilst Burmese, Thai and Sri Lankan Theravadin teachers offered teachings in their traditions. At the same time, western forms of Buddhism, such as Sangharakshita's FWBO and Lama Govinda's *Arya Maitreya Mandala* were beginning to take shape.

The academic study of Buddhism also progressed apace. More and more texts were translated into English and other European languages and academic specialists began to work at rendering some of the more abstruse points of Buddhist doctrine into terms readily accessible to western thinkers. Never before in Buddhist history had so much doctrinal material been available at the same time – buried texts from central Asia were coming to light, and these could be compared to later recensions from Tibet, China and Japan, as well as earlier material which had survived in Pali. Buddhologists set to work making comparative studies and the beginning of a scholastically accurate Buddhist 'higher criticism' began to emerge and with it the possibility of sifting the Canonical Scriptures and dating the different layers of material they contain.

For religions which are founded primarily in belief, such scholastic delving can appear to be a threat, but for Buddhism, founded as it is in experience rather than belief, the results of scholastic analysis can only be welcomed for the clarity they bring to the Buddhist Scriptures. By knowing more accurately the chronology of the development of the Buddhist tradition we can come to a clearer understanding of why certain teachings were given when they were, and this can help us to see how we can apply them in our own practice. Thus, increasingly, the academic study of Buddhism has come to be carried out by practising Buddhists, whose analysis is motivated as much by a desire to shed light on practice as it is by abstract scholarly interest.

By the mid–1980s a number of westerners were beginning to assume significant spiritual responsibilities in the Buddhist groups within which they functioned. Several key Asian teachers had died, their places being taken by western successors, and other teachers began to make plans for handing over their spiritual responsibilities.

Today many hundreds of western Buddhist teachers carry out their work at some of the thousands of Buddhist centres in Europe, the United States, Australia, New Zealand and South Africa. Many of these teachers have come to know one another as personal friends, and the dialogues which are taking place between, for example, an English *bhikkhu* practising in the Thai Theravada tradition and an American woman teaching Soto Zen, are helping to expand the western understanding of what the Buddhist tradition as a whole is all about.

For we in the west today stand as heirs to the whole Buddhist tradition and need not identify ourselves exclusively with one or another of the many Asian Buddhist forms. Experienced western Buddhist practitioners can come to an informed appreciation of the diverse merits of all the different schools and, by empathetically examining the tradition as a whole, can begin to distinguish what is essential from what is peripheral – thus freeing the central, liberative teachings of the Buddha from the weight of later cultural encrustation.

Our brief survey of the history of Buddhism in the west has brought us right up to the present. But what of the future? What will a truly *western* form of Buddhism look like? Of course it is too early to say, but a start has been made. I will therefore conclude by looking at a Buddhist group whose primary intention is to integrate Buddhism into western culture – or rather, western culture into Buddhism. This is the Friends of the Western Buddhist Order, which was founded by an English Buddhist, Sangharakshita, in 1967.

Born into an ordinary working class family in London in 1925, childhood illness kept the young Sangharakshita from school, and so he educated himself, working his way through the major classics of English literature, ancient Rome and Greece, eventually embarking on the classical works of the oriental religions. At the age of 16, upon reading the Diamond Sutra, together with the Sutra of Hui-Neng, he was propelled into a profound mystical experience, and he realized that he was a Buddhist.

Conscripted in 1943, the war took him to Sri Lanka and India, where, with the cessation of hostilities, he simply walked away from the army – shaving his head and adopting the ochre-dyed robe of a homeless ascetic, he 'went forth'. Living on alms, he wandered the roads of India in search of spiritual sustenance – a search which led to his eventual ordination in 1950 as a Theravadin *bhikkhu*.

His then teacher, the *Tipitaka* master Ven. Jagdish Kashyap, suggested that he base himself in Kalimpong, an idyllic hill town near to the Indo-Tibetan border, 'and work for the good of Buddhism'. He did so for many years and, being in Kalimpong, was well-placed when the first Tibetan *lamas* began to pour out of Tibet into exile in India, and he received teachings and initiations from many of them.

In 1964 Sangharakshita was invited back to England to help establish the Dharma there, but the genteel English Buddhist establishment of the time wasn't ready for anyone quite so radical. The kind of person they wanted, one luminary suggested, would be the 'Buddhist equivalent of the vicar of Hampstead' and the time soon came for a parting of ways. Realizing that for Buddhism to truly flourish in the west a new approach was needed, in 1967, in a tiny basement shrine-room beneath an oriental antiques shop in London, Sangharakshita founded the FWBO. Since then, the FWBO has grown into an international Buddhist movement with activities conducted in about 130 towns and cities around the world.

In many respects the FWBO is just like any of the other Buddhist groups which can be found in almost all the cities of the west today: it offers courses and classes in meditation and Buddhism, celebrates the usual Buddhist festivals and draws for its teaching on the broad range of Buddhist canonical literature. But there are some elements of the FWBO which make it particularly interesting when considering what a truly western form of Buddhism might be. For it consciously addresses itself to issues which are peculiar to the contemporary western situation. What is the relationship of Buddhism to western culture? How is one's practice of the Dharma affected by contemporary western economic and political realities? How does a Christian (or even post-Christian) upbringing affect one's attitude to ethics? How can one combine the responsibilities of being a single parent with one's desire to practise the Dharma? These are just a few of the vast complex of issues which arise as a result of the interaction between Buddhism and the particular social and psychological conditions which prevail in the west today.

Whilst the history of Asian Buddhism is largely the history of Buddhist monasticism, western Buddhism appears to be moving in a different direction. With few exceptions, most of the Buddhist organizations in the west today concern themselves with teaching different varieties of 'lay-Buddhism', trying to create some kind of accommodation between the demands of Buddhist practice on the one hand, and those of the modern western lifestyle on the other.

The FWBO tries to take this one stage further. It asserts that questions of lifestyle need to be subsumed to questions of spiritual commitment. For although it is clear that a spiritually committed householder is Dharmically better off than a spiritually apathetic monk, the FWBO also recognizes the impact that one's style of life inevitably has on the possibilities for spiritual practice. It is no easy matter to hold down a regular job, be a parent, keep up a regular meditation practice, attend a Buddhist class each week and get away for six weeks of retreat each year! For this reason the FWBO has established a number of institutions whose primary purpose is to make it possible for people to lead a viable Buddhist lifestyle in the context of modern western life.

At the heart of the FWBO is the Western Buddhist Order itself. This is a new Sangha – a spiritual community of men and women who have effectively committed themselves to orienting their lives around the Three Jewels. The Order is neither lay nor monastic. Some of its members choose to be celibate, others not. Some live with their families and hold regular jobs, others live in single-sex residential spiritual communities, work in FWBO Right Livelihood businesses or teach at FWBO centres. What they all have in common, however, is an effective commitment to living in accordance with the values embodied in the Three Jewels.

Around the Order is a much wider circle of Friends, who have different levels of involvement with the FWBO, from beginners to those training for ordination. Friends may attend just a few FWBO activities a year, or they may live and work alongside Order members, participating full-time in the FWBO project to find ways of creating a new western Buddhist culture – even a new society.

Unwilling to depend on the economic support of those who

are not spiritually committed, the FWBO has developed a number of Right Livelihood businesses. Surplus profits from the businesses help to fund the work of the FWBO. Motivated by that fact, people work on the basis of 'give what you can, take what you need'. Living simply, often communally, remuneration depends on people's actual needs, not on the level of responsibility they take.

Believing that we cannot progress spiritually by cutting ourselves off from our cultural roots and adopting a whole new eastern culture, but rather that, rooted in western culture, western Buddhists can play a part in the development of the culture itself, the FWBO encourages its members to investigate western art forms for themselves, to find in them what resonates with the Dharma. There are several Buddhist Arts Centres associated with FWBO Buddhist centres in the UK. Plays, oratorios, paintings, sculptures and other works have been produced, and there are regular workshops given over to investigating one or another aspect of the western cultural tradition.

Around the London Buddhist Centre, the FWBO's largest UK centre, a kind of urban 'Buddhist village' has come into being. There are around a dozen residential communities, several Right Livelihood businesses, a complementary health centre, an arts centre, a Buddhist library and the Buddhist centre itself, which runs a programme of around 40 different meetings each week, both at the centre and elsewhere. Pervading the whole 'village' is an atmosphere of spiritual friendship, for perhaps above all this is what people really need to help them to grow and develop in the modern, emotionally alienated environment.

But the FWBO doesn't see itself as simply providing a friendly supportive matrix for a few people who have a common interest in Buddhism. For it recognizes that the world in which it functions is in a very sorry state indeed. And the task which the FWBO has set for itself is in fact the task of all modern Buddhists, for the Buddha taught the Dharma, not so that a few people might enjoy happier mental states. He taught it for the sake of a world which is constantly being consumed by the flames of greed, hatred and delusion.

We live in a world of gross material inequality, ecological despoliation, political and psychological oppression, personal isolation and emotional alienation. And the underlying cause of the devastating waste of human potential which we see all around is nothing but spiritual ignorance. Trapped in worlds of delusive fantasy, driven by the forces of greed, hatred, spiritual ignorance, we all act again and again in ways which cause ourselves and others to suffer. We act like this because we are fundamentally spiritually ignorant and we will continue to do so until spiritual truth, the Dharma, informs every dimension of our lives.

Spiritual principles have social implications. Western Buddhists should therefore seek to make the Dharma known as widely as possible; to find ways of living in modern society which support the individual's practice of the Dharma; and, as a result, to begin to change the world for the better. The task is urgent – for unless western culture, which is the dominant culture of our age, begins to be informed by values which take us beyond our immense thirst for immediate gratification, then it is hard to see how things could not but get very much worse on an over-crowded and under-resourced planet, so much marked by human suffering.

We in the west today have access to enormous riches. Collectively, we command technological and material resources far beyond the dreams of our ancestors. Behind us stands our western cultural heritage, thousands of years old, rich in goodness, truth and beauty. Ahead of us lies – what? If we can bring about a marriage, a blending of Buddhism and what is best in western culture, the future might be glorious indeed.

References

1) Yampolsky, Philip B. *Selected Writings of Nichiren*, New York, 1990.

2) Adapted from Bishop, Peter. *Dreams of Power: Tibetan Buddhism and the Western Imagination*, The Athlone Press, 1993.

3) Batchelor, Stephen. *The Awakening of the West: the Encounter of Buddhism and Western Culture*, Aquarian, 1994.

4) Ibid.

In the same series. . .

PRINCIPLES OF TAROT

EVELYNE AND TERRY DONALDSON

Tarot has fascinated people for hundreds of years, but at times the symbolism can be difficult to relate to our contemporary lives. This introductory guide demystifies the tarot and clearly explains:

- the meaning of each card

- how to do a reading for yourself and other people

- how to use the tarot as a tool for personal development

- easy ways of gaining a deeper understanding of this ancient art

Evelyne and Terry Donaldson are highly experienced tarot teachers and readers. They run the London Tarot Training Centre. Terry Donaldson is the author of *Step by Step Tarot*, also published by Thorsons, co-creator of the *Dragon Tarot* deck and *Wyvern, the game of Dragons, Dragon-Slayers and Treasure.*

PRINCIPLES OF NLP

JOSEPH O'CONNOR AND IAN MCDERMOTT

Neuro-Linguistic Programming (NLP) is the psychology of excellence. It is based on the practical skills that are used by all good communicators to obtain excellent results. These skills are invaluable for personal and professional development. This introductory guide explains:

- what NLP is

- how to use it in your life personally, spiritually and professionally

- how to understand body language

- how to achieve excellence in everything that you do

Joseph O'Connor is a trainer, consultant and software designer. He is the author of the bestselling *Introducing NLP* and several other titles, including *Successful Selling with NLP* and *Training with NLP*.

Ian McDermott is a certified trainer with the Society of Neuro-Linguistic Programming. He is the Director of Training for International Teaching Seminars, the leading NLP training organization in the UK.

PRINCIPLES OF
SELF-HEALING

DAVID LAWSON

In these high pressure times we are in need of ways of relaxing and gaining a sense of happiness and peace. There are many skills and techniques that we can master to bring healing and well-being to our minds and bodies.

This introductory guide includes:

- visualizations to encourage our natural healing process

- affirmations to guide and inspire

- ways of developing the latent power of the mind

- techniques for gaining a deeper understanding of yourself and others

David Lawson is a teacher, healer and writer. He has worked extensively with Louise Hay, author of *You Can Heal Your Life*, and runs workshops throughout the world. He is the author of several books on the subject, including *I See Myself in Perfect Health*, also published by Thorsons.

PRINCIPLES OF HYPNOTHERAPY

VERA PEIFFER

Interest in hypnotherapy has grown rapidly over the last few years. Many people are realizing that it is an effective way to solve problems such as mental and emotional trauma, anxiety, depression, phobias and confidence problems, and eliminate unwanted habits such as smoking. This introductory guide explains:

- what hypnotherapy is

- how it works

- what its origins are

- what to expect when you go for treatment

- how to find a reputable hypnotherapist

Vera Peiffer is a leading authority on hypnotherapy. She is a psychologist in private practice in West London specializing in analytical hypnotherapy and a member of the Corporation of Advanced Hypnotherapy.

PRINCIPLES OF PAGANISM

VIVIANNE CROWLEY

Interest in Paganism is steadily increasing and, while rooted in ancient tradition, it is a living religious movement. With its reverence for all creation, it reflects our current concern for the planet. This introductory guide explains:

- what Paganism is

- the different Pagan paths

- what Pagans do

- how to live as a Pagan

Vivianne Crowley is the author of the bestselling *Wicca: The Old Religion in the New Millennium*. She is a priestess, a teacher of the Pagan way and a leading figure in western Paganism. She has a doctorate in psychology and has trained in transpersonal therapy.

PRINCIPLES OF
NUTRITIONAL THERAPY

LINDA LAZARIDES

Environmental pollutants and the use of antibiotics and other drugs cause changes in the body which can affect its ability to absorb and assimilate nutrients. Widespread nutritional deficiencies causing much chronic illness have resulted from this in our society. Nutritional therapists, complementary medicine practitioners working with special dies and vitamins, are often able to cure illnesses such a eczema, chronic fatigue, premenstrual syndrome, irritable bowel syndrome, hyperactivity and migraine.

This introductory guide explains:

- how deficiencies occur

- how nutritional therapy works

- which key illnesses the therapy can fight

Linda Lazarides is Director of the Society for the Promotion of Nutritional Therapy. She is a practising nutritional therapist with several years of working with a GP. She is an advisor to the Institute of Complementary Medicine and BACUP and is on the advisory panel of *Here's Health* magazine.

PRINCIPLES OF
THE ENNEAGRAM

KAREN WEBB

There is a growing fascination with the Enneagram – the ancient uncannily accurate model of personality types linking personality to spirit. Most people can recognize themselves as one of the nine archetypes. This introduction to the subject explains:

- the characteristics of the nine types

- how the system works

- ways of understanding your own personality

- how to discover your true potential and attain it

- ways to enhance your relationships

Karen Webb is an experienced Enneagram teacher, counsellor and workshop leader. She has introduced many people to the system and guided them in using the information to change their lives. She has been employed by many large companies as a management consultant.

PRINCIPLES OF TAROT	0 7225 3217 2	£5.99
PRINCIPLES OF NLP	0 7225 3195 8	£5.99
PRINCIPLES OF THE ENNEAGRAM	0 7225 3191 5	£5.99
PRINCIPLES OF HYPNOTHERAPY	0 7225 3242 3	£5.99
PRINCIPLES OF PAGANISM	1 85538 507 4	£5.99
PRINCIPLES OF NUTRITIONAL THERAPY	0 7225 3285 7	£5.99
PRINCIPLES OF SELF-HEALING	1 85538 486 8	£5.99

All these books are available from your local bookseller or can be ordered direct from the publishers.

To order direct just tick the titles you want and fill in the form below:

Name:

Address:

Postcode:

Send to Thorsons Mail Order, Dept 3, HarperCollinsPublishers, Westerhill Road, Bishopbriggs, Glasgow G64 2QT.

Please enclose a cheque or postal order or your authority to debit your Visa/Access account —

Credit card no:

Expiry date:

Signature:

— up to the value of the cover price plus:
UK & BFPO: Add £1.00 for the first book and 25p for each additional book ordered.

Overseas orders including Eire: Please add £2.95 service charge. Books will be sent by surface mail but quotes for airmail dispatches will be given on request.

24–HOUR TELEPHONE ORDERING SERVICE FOR ACCESS/VISA CARD-HOLDERS — TEL: 0141 772 2281.